A PROVEN BLUEPRINT FOR SUCCESSFUL
PROFESSIONALS TO OVERCOME SEX
AND PORN ADDICTION

THE

HIGH

ACHIEVER'S

GUIDE TO

SEX

ADDICTION

RECOVERY

A PROVEN BLUEPRINT FOR SUCCESSFUL
PROFESSIONALS TO OVERCOME SEX
AND PORN ADDICTION

THE

HIGH

ACHIEVER'S

GUIDE TO

SEX

ADDICTION

RECOVERY

DR. ROLAND COCHRUN

Printed in the United States of America
First Printing, 2025
ISBN: 979-8-9852063-1-9
Library of Congress Number: 2024927506

Summit Press Publishers
P.O. Box 1356
Intervale, New Hampshire 03845

For information about special discounts available for bulk purchase, workshops, retreats, and webinars associated with this book or offered by Roland Cochrun, please contact him at www.successfuladdict.com

This book is dedicated to my wife.
Thank you for staying with me and giving me a
second chance. It's a big ask after everything that
I have done to you.

Table of Contents

Introduction

There are a ton of great books about sex and porn addiction. So, why did I feel the need to write another? Because I believe much of the sex addiction recovery industry is unorganized, inefficient, and incomplete. It's an industry that continues to lean heavily on faith-based treatment approaches and archaic recovery practices—that applies substance addiction principles to an addiction entirely different from substance addiction. With that, it's no wonder you'll often read that it takes men a little over two years to fully recover.

Sure, some things take time; and addiction recovery is definitely one of those things. Yet, time does not heal an addiction; the recovery work does the healing.

I know from personal experience. As a high achiever in almost every area of my life, I approached my sex addiction with the same tenacity as everything else I sought to accomplish. I had money, free time, and a deep desire to stay married to my beautiful wife, soulmate, and best friend. Yet, despite having access to everything I needed to achieve a speedy recovery, it wasn't speedy at all.

Every "specialist" had a different approach to recovery. There was no plan in place. No roadmap to follow. All I could do was go to weekly therapy appointments, 12-step meetings, call a random guy who is apparently "my sponsor," and keep signing up for sex addiction treatment intensives. Sometimes I would experience a breakthrough, other times it seemed as though I was sliding backward, and it was taking a toll on my marriage.

After about eight months into recovery, I started to lose faith in the sex addiction industry. With the hundreds of different opinions and lack of research to support almost any of the treatment strategies, I found myself lost and discouraged. How could it be? I had a deep desire to recover, all the motivation in the world to save my marriage, access to some of the best therapists and treatment programs, and free time to put into the homework after hours. Yet, I was stuck. I was not relapsing, but it was a true possibility.

If you are reading this book, my guess is that you do not consider yourself out of the woods yet. You and/or your wife know that you still struggle with sexually compulsive thinking. Maybe you find yourself looking at women on social media. Maybe you find yourself looking at pornography and unable to stop. Maybe you woke up next to a woman who you barely know. Maybe you are paying women for nude photos. Maybe you are paying women to have sex with you. Maybe you relapsed and your wife caught you. Or, you haven't relapsed yet, but you know it could happen if the wrong situation presented itself.

Maybe you've asked yourself these types of questions:

- How do I save my marriage after all the damage and lying?

- What is the perfect recovery plan and how do I set it up?

- How do I change my mind so that this addiction stops haunting me?

- I've tried recovery before and got sober, but I never stopped wanting to act out sexually; will it ever completely go away?

- How can I make my wife feel confident that I'm doing all I can and that this won't be a problem again?

- I see men relapsing all the time; is this addiction ever something that someone can overcome?

- Will my marriage ever go back to what it was before?

- Will my wife ever trust me again?

They're common questions. It's easy to see why men ask them. The consequences of this addiction are vast and damaging: Divorce, losing custody of your children, destroying your reputation, contracting a sexually transmitted disease, giving that disease to your wife, or getting arrested for soliciting a prostitute or visiting a massage parlour.

Even if you can hide your addiction, you still must deal with the constant hiding, lying, and deception. Knowing your wife is blind to the things you are doing to her; knowing your kids would lose all respect for you if they were ever to find out about your secret sexual life.

Regardless of the magnitude of your sexual behaviour, if you are reading this book, you know you must dive deeper into recovery if you want to get these compulsive sexual behaviors out of your life.

Chances are good, you've already tried. In doing so, you discovered how hard it is to do everything that is required. You know you need deep connections with other sex addicts. Your therapist, addiction research, and the men who have achieved sobriety all tell you that finding a group of men to recover with is the single most important aspect of achieving long-term recovery. You need to find like-minded men you admire and respect—men with whom you enjoy spending time and of whom you value opinions. You need to feel they understand what it's like to be you and that they are invested in your recovery. Such connections are hard to find in the real world; they are even more difficult to find in the sex addiction world.

You've tried going to 12-step meetings, only to find them relatively unmotivating for a higher level of commitment, since many of the guys struggle to maintain sobriety. Outside of peer support, you keep going to therapy week after week hoping that your therapist finally "cracks the code" and magically makes you sober.

In reality, getting down to the root cause of your sex addiction takes work. Showing up to therapy and expecting your therapist to "fix" you is not how recovery works. Most of the work will happen on your clock. It's up to you to bring the pertinent information to your therapy appointments so it can be processed. But how do you discover what needs to be worked on in between therapy appointments; how are you supposed to speed up your recovery if you have no idea what to do next?

There you are—putting your life on hold, your marriage on the line, banking on free 12-step meetings, weekly therapy appointments, calling your sponsor to get you sober and change your brain—when it finally hits you: *Is this actually going to work? Is this really the best recovery plan there is?*

The answer is no.

If you're like me, getting these sexual behaviors out of your life is important to you. Sex addiction is tarnishing your legacy, harming your relationships, and stealing hours of your life from you each week. Relying on a slow and inefficient plan is unacceptable.

This book is intended to help.

As you work through the process, remember: They call it recovery for a reason. You are recovering what was lost. When you are in the midst of your addiction it's hard to see it that way, but give it some time. What you gain will make all the pain and struggle insignificant in comparison.

1

My Addiction Story

I got caught. I wish I could tell you that I came clean on my own, and told my wife the truth, but I didn't. Neither one of us knew anything about sex addiction. The closest we came was tied to the Tiger Woods scandal. Even then, it quickly turned into a joke about how they fabricated the term so Tiger could shift the blame and salvage his reputation.

Now, I love my wife more than words can describe. It would take multiple lifetimes to find another woman like her. She's stunningly beautiful; she's smart and capable and in no way "stuck" with me. She could be with any man she wants. So, when she discovered my sexual behavior outside of our marriage, I was willing to do anything to save the relationship. I knew there was an expiration date on her forgiveness. So, I had to act fast. With each passing day, the chance of divorce increased.

Regrettably, I lied to cover it up and tried to convince her this was an isolated incident. The problem with lies is that they don't hold up. My wife felt in her gut that something was wrong. Eventually, she bought a book about sexual betrayal, and that is when everything came crashing down.

She told me she wanted to see a Certified Sex Addiction Therapist (CSAT) and go through a "full therapeutic disclosure"—a therapy process where the cheating partner documents a complete history of his sexual behavior. Some wives choose not to hear it all; my wife wanted to know everything. At that moment, I knew I was fucked and that there was a good chance she was going to leave me.

In my head, my extramarital behavior was "not that bad." Sure, there was some confessing to do, but certainly my missteps were not as egregious as that of other guys.

I was mistaken.

As I sat down to record everything, there was more than I thought. Much more. Disclosure was one of the most painful experiences of my life. Reading that document to her in front of our therapists is a day I will not forget. The look in her eyes as I kept reading all the things that I did during our marriage is forever burned into my memory.

I still read that disclosure document in disbelief. *How could I do all those things?* Of course, that's the whole point of a therapeutic disclosure: to own what you did, face the consequences, and pray she gives you another chance.

In all my previous relationships, I would have run. Why go through the pain, humiliation, and guilt? But something was different about Lauren. She was worth fighting for.

The two years that followed disclosure were not easy. We were both in our early thirties; we didn't have kids. It would have been far easier to simply walk away and start new relationships. She could find a guy who wouldn't betray her trust—someone who would cherish her and not make her feel small, disregarded, or easily replaced; I could find a woman who would trust me to take care of her—someone free of horrible memories of me and what I have done to her.

Somehow, our marriage survived. She chose me and I chose her. To this day, healing our marriage was the hardest thing either of us have ever done. For her, the first year was hell on earth. For me, the second year had me wanting to quit almost every other week. We trusted the process. Luckily, it worked.

Harder Than They Make It Sound

Two years before my wife discovered my sexual behavior, I sold my first business to a Wall Street investment company. Which means I had unlimited time and money to attack this addiction. That, combined with an intense desire to save my marriage, put me in a favorable position to accelerate my addiction recovery.

That's not how it went.

The sex addiction industry was all over the place. There was very little research to support any of the available treatment strategies. Yet my marriage was imploding; I had to act fast.

I followed my therapist's plan to a tee: attended therapy, went to multiple 12-step meetings each week, listened to every podcast, and bought every book. It still wasn't enough for my wife. She felt I was just checking off the boxes and not really in recovery, which frustrated the hell out of me. *What more did she want?* Between it all, I was spending nearly fifteen hours a week doing recovery work.

But as much as I wanted to disagree with her, I knew there was some truth to what she was saying. In business, when I really want something, I find a way to make it happen—even if it means inventing a completely new strategy. Week after week I attended therapy, but it seemed the same old thing over and over again. I was learning about recovery, but not necessarily recovering.

There's a big difference between talking about what needs to be done and implementing a plan that will actually work. It's akin to college and entrepreneurship: college exposes you to a bunch of different theories and ideas; entrepreneurship requires a viable plan that can be measured and modified. The first five months of my sex addiction recovery felt like college—a whole lot of time and money spent with very little action towards creating meaningful change.

Yes, I acted sober, but I wasn't recovered, and my wife knew it. Stopping the sexual behavior was not enough for her. She wanted to *feel* the change in me. I wanted the same thing, but the current plan was moving far too slowly, and I feared our marriage wouldn't make it.

I had been in the position before, in business. For years, I read books, attended conferences, and hired consultants. I had the knowledge to succeed; what I needed was a way to connect the dots and reap the benefits. That's when I stumbled across a mastermind group . . .

A business mastermind is a small group of like-minded people who share a common problem and want to achieve the same result. They typically meet over

Zoom each week, gather in person a few times each year, and have a platform to support each other in between meetings. The group is facilitated by a person who has accomplished what the other group members are hoping to achieve.

The concept is highly effective when it comes to accelerating results. And the reason I had been in multiple groups over the years. All of them helped me build multi-million-dollar businesses in a relatively short period of time. So, when I discovered I had a sex addiction, I went looking for a mastermind group that could help me accelerate the process of rewiring my brain.

It didn't exist.

The closest thing I could find were sex addiction intensives and 12-step meetings. Neither of which came close to the effectiveness of a mastermind group. There was very little structure, no plan, poor accountability, and a total lack of urgency. Many of the sex addiction programs are faith-based, which is a bit off-putting to a guy like me. As a medical professional, I want facts, research, and scientifically proven treatment methods. To me, religion and mental health should be kept separate.

It was also very difficult for me to find men with whom I could connect. As a high achiever and entrepreneur, I typically connect better with those who think the same way I do, who have similar life experiences. Such men were rarely ever in a 12-step meeting; even if I found one, it was difficult to meet regularly enough to form a real connection.

Before long, frustration took over the recovery process. It was everything it shouldn't be: unstructured, dull, and incredibly slow. Everyone seemed to be "waiting for change." I hate waiting. So does my wife.

If I learned anything from being in business mastermind groups, it's that the process needs to be organized, efficient, fun, and done in a group. I made this happen for my recovery—and I wrote this book to help you do the same.

It Started When I Was Young

As with any addiction story, it's not complete if you don't begin where it all started . . .

I was born the middle child of three—with a brother who arrived seven years before, and a sister who arrived three years after me. Growing up, our household was incredibly religious; the church was everything to our parents and they expected us to feel the same. My brother lived up to their expectations. He was an Eagle Scout, valedictorian in high school, and the president of pretty much every scholastic club you can imagine. Not only did he follow all the religious rules set by the church, he served a two-year mission spreading the gospel in Spain before attending college.

In other words, he set the bar high when it came to pleasing my parents. His was a tough act to follow. Not to mention, it was an act I did not care to follow. A life spent following the rules of others was unappealing to me. I hated the way church leaders and other kids treated me. They knew I was not like them, and they made that very clear. Constantly, I was told my actions would not get me to heaven, that I was setting a bad example for my little sister. My own parents wanted me to act more like my "perfect" older brother.

When I said I didn't want to attend church, they dismissed my wishes and forced me to attend. They threatened my freedom by not allowing me to see my friends on the weekends if I did not go to church and youth group every week. I felt unheard and unseen. In psychology, this is often referred to as a "one-down" position. When you are led to believe that your emotions and opinions are less valuable than those of others.

Before long, I was lying to my parents. If they knew what I was really doing, they would punish me. The older I got, the more the lies escalated. To cover my tracks, I got good at lying . . . so good that I always got away with it. At last, I was in the "one-up" position. I knew something they didn't know. To this day, I don't like people telling me what to do or what to believe and it's something I recognized about myself by the age of nine.

My parents did not understand. To them, living life the way they instructed was the right way—the only way. Believing or doing something different was unacceptable and choosing to do so led to punishment.

So, my childhood was spent walking the line between being punished and doing what my parents told me to do. To preserve my freedom, I did the bare minimum required by my parents and hid my true desires and aspirations. In doing so, I began to live a double life—one life for them, and one life for me—thus learning to violate my integrity.

While never their intent, they taught me life is about pleasing others. They never took the time to ask how I felt, what excited me, what captured my attention, or what I wanted to do. They were only interested in seeing that I believed in their religion and grew up to be financially stable.

Most parents want their children to succeed, to accomplish great things, and go to heaven. *But what about what I want and need?* Because that never factored in, I felt more like a pet than a person.

As a result, I spent most of my childhood fantasizing about what I would become after moving out of my parent's house. Impressing my parents was simply never going to happen, so my only hope was to learn how to impress everyone else.

I became a full-time people pleaser, starting with my friends' rich parents. I got good grades, practiced good manners, saved my money, and lived for the moments when they would turn to my friend and say, "Why can't you be more like Roland?"

Then I turned fifteen and discovered bodybuilding.

It's hard to do anything impressive when you're a teenager, but bodybuilding turned heads. It captured the attention of everyone at school, including the teachers. The discipline and dedication required even managed to impress my parents.

It became an obsession. At the time, there was only one other kid in the whole state of Oregon competing in bodybuilding. For the first time in my life, I felt unique and special. So, even though I didn't particularly care for the sport itself (it was incredibly demanding and required a significant amount of sacrifice), I loved the attention it awarded me. After never being able to impress my parents, bodybuilding finally gave me a place in the world.

Unfortunately, the sport requires the use of steroids and hormones if you plan to go professional. That was something that I was not willing to do. But it was too painful to give up until I had a proven replacement.

That's when I discovered money.

Intoxicated by Success

I quit bodybuilding upon entering my doctorate program. It was an easy transition as my obsession shifted towards school and eventually opening my own practice. Much like bodybuilding, money can turn heads. So, I became engulfed in becoming the best; I attended every conference that would help me achieve my goals as a practitioner and accelerate my success in business.

Of course, my world was much bigger than it was in high school. It was harder to impress everyone, since each person had a different definition of impressive. There are seven billion people on earth; rather than recognizing the insanity of trying to impress all of them, I pressed forward and kept trying.

I lived life like it was a contest: impress more people, be more important. By the time I was thirty, I had become something of a sausage—a blend of everything I believed other people thought impressive. There was no interest in being authentic.

As a Rolex-wearing sausage who lacked any sense of true self, there was nothing stopping me from acting compulsively because I refused to recognize my talent and fulfill my potential. In psychology, it's called self-actualization, and it's a pre-programmed need. Which means it cannot be ignored without dire consequences. The pain I felt every single day was not because I was inadequate. It was because I was straying further and further away from who I was supposed to be.

My pathological desire to be superior, respected, and admired was at the core of my sexually compulsive behavior. As a boy who often questioned his value, I cared very much about becoming someone people considered impressive. I paid close attention to male celebrities who people admired. They always seemed to be in superior positions and had more money than other men. I also noticed that they got attention from attractive women and oftentimes were able to easily convince them to have sex. So, when I started chasing career success, I used these men as my measure.

Success was never measured by how I felt inside. It was always gauged by what other people were saying and thinking about me. No wonder my wife used to feel like my second priority. She was right. My need for attention and validation was so strong that it often overrode everything (and everyone) else in my life. I wanted men to envy me and women to sleep with me.

And just like that, my sexual behavior moved beyond pornography. With attention and validation being the goals, my compulsive mind preferred real women over virtual images. Like all addictions, the need got worse. Eventually, I was doing things I told myself I would never do.

The fantasy of becoming somebody important turned into an obsession. I was convinced that life was meaningless if you were not one of "the best." There was constant pressure every day: be better looking, be smarter, have more, be more. From the moment I awoke, the pressure to succeed weighed on me. Obsessing, daydreaming, planning, strategizing, learning, and thinking of ways to improve filled my mind.

Happiness did not play into the equation. All that mattered was that I was admired, respected, and appreciated. The moment that no longer held true—the moment I was no longer noticed for my success—was the moment I quit and switched to something that would capture the attention of others.

It was more than a goal or desire. I *needed* to be more. There was no off switch to the constant need to excel. Even on vacation, I dreamt about achieving more, succeeding more, and having more. It was exhausting.

The constant need for more paired with the insatiable desire for attention is a lethal combination. My brain convinced me that getting validation from others was the only way I would feel good. Unfortunately, it came at the cost of compromising my values. Mainly, cheating on my wife.

The Support I Needed

Sex addiction was but one of many addictions. While I never became addicted to drugs or alcohol, I lived most of my life addicted to thought processes rather than actually living life.

Even after seeking help, I wanted people to see me as successful, superior, attractive, and accomplished. Sure, I was sexually sober. I wasn't watching porn or having sex outside of my marriage. But I was craving attention and interactions that could (and nearly did) destroy my marriage. I wanted attractive women to want me and married women to wish they could be with me instead of their husbands; I wanted to know I could sleep with them if I wanted to and that they wanted to sleep with me. I believed those things would bring me the attention, validation, control, wealth, and superiority that would raise me to the top.

That's not how it happened. The men who complemented me were not the ones I sought to impress; the women who wanted to sleep with me were shallow and only wanted me for my looks and the digits in my bank account. It was not true respect and admiration. It was all a game, and I fell for it. There I was with millions in the bank and six-pack abs, only to find myself feeling even less respected and admired than I was before.

I wasn't alive. There was nothing human about me. And since this world is made for humans, I could never seem to make it work for me. There always seemed to be something missing . . . my humanity.

When my sexual behaviors were discovered by my wife, I could not understand how I had gotten there. I had told myself that I would never do the things I did, but I did them. I never thought I would be the husband who did this to his wife, until I was that husband.

Despite the fact that I was in meetings, men's groups, therapy, and treatment programs for most of my recovery, I found myself alone. I had to invent my own recovery plan.

So, I hired some of the best addiction specialists in the country—and ended up working with many professionals outside of the sex addiction world. They were not Certified Sex Addiction Therapists, but smart psychologists who had experience working with highly successful males. And it worked!

With their help, I was able to get to the root cause of my sexually compulsive behavior. I was able to discover my triggers and remove them from my life. After years of struggle, I was finally able to find all the pieces needed to make a full recovery.

Which brings me to the writing of this book. I decided to sit down and write down what I learned, so you might learn it quicker. My hope is that by reading its pages, you will be able to make a full recovery, not in years, but in a matter of months.

2

It's Not About Sex

If you haven't already realized, sex addiction has very little to do with sex. It is a result of compulsive thinking patterns, developed over time. If you don't identify all aspects of your compulsive thought processes, this addiction may never go away.

The following pages provide a framework with which to examine the thought processes you are chasing. You will discover what your brain is trying to accomplish by using sex, porn, or affairs and why it has chosen sex/women as its preferred method; how this addiction happened and what you can do to change it; and the proven process to change your mind so that you no longer act in a way that harms your future.

My hope is that you not only stop your unwanted sexual behavior but stop wanting to do it in the first place—that after reading this book, you will see how you can strengthen the sober mind to the point where your addict mind doesn't stand a chance.

Men often say to me, "I can act sober, but will these thoughts and desires ever go away?" The answer is yes, and this book will show you how. But first, you need to understand why recovery is different for you.

Recovery is Different for High Achievers

High achievers are driven individuals who achieve above-average success due to their high level of commitment and determination. To them, the fear of failure does not compare to the fear of never living up to their full potential. Different from the general population, they think differently, spend their time differently, and live a very different lifestyle.

While most people spend their lives dreaming about the perfect life, high achievers spend their lives making their dreams reality. They have the drive to reach their goals and a continuous desire for more. They focus on the end result more than the current moment, constantly planning their next move and searching for the fastest way forward. They value efficiency and a thoughtful plan—personality traits that typically result in accelerated career success.

Culturally-speaking (especially in America), high achievers tend to operate as a separate race of people. They maintain the same lifestyle, live in the same neighborhoods, engage in the same social activities. They spend most of their time around other successful people at networking events, business conferences, and social clubs.

While they are often criticized for separating themselves from those who are less successful, exclusion is not necessarily their intent. Much like anyone else, they simply enjoy spending time with those with whom they can relate. They also tend to have more time off work and access to more resources, allowing them to participate in activities the general population may not be able to enjoy. They are generally well-traveled; they've seen things many other people have not. Their life experiences change the way they think and how they see the world. For these reasons, they tend to feel more seen, accepted, and understood when hanging out with like-minded people.

High achievers make up 2% of the population.[1] Because they are a minority group and have what appears

1 Henryk Krajewski, "The Cold, Hard Truth Behind How Many 'Star Employees' You Really Have, *Forbes*, January 2, 2020, https://www.forbes.com/councils/forbescoachescouncil/2020/01/02/the-cold-hard-truth-behind-how-many-star-employees-you-really-have/.

to be a "great life," they are often ignored or overlooked. For obvious reasons, most psychology books and research focus on 98% of the general population. The sex addiction field is no different.

Much of the sex addiction literature available today is inapplicable to a high achiever's particular compulsive sexual behavior. Those at 12-step meetings often struggle with issues to which a high achiever simply cannot relate because they do not settle for mediocrity; most of them are not in unpleasant situations for long. Rather than make excuses, they look for solutions. For this reason, it can be incredibly challenging for high-achieving males to find other like-minded men to connect with in recovery.

For example, in the book *Facing the Shadow* (which is considered the bible for sex addiction), Patrick Carnes identifies the core belief of the sex addict as, "I am basically a bad, unworthy person."[2]

Therapists tend to echo Carnes, saying there's an underlying belief of worthlessness for sex addicts. While this may be true for the general population, it's not necessarily the case for high achievers. Those who attend my sex addiction retreats are successful lawyers, surgeons, business professionals, executives, celebrities, professional ath-

---

2 Patrick Carnes, *Facing the Shadow: Starting Sexual and Relationship Recovery* (Gentle Path Press, 2015).

letes, and entrepreneurs, who all report feeling capable and worthy of accomplishing great things. When asked if they felt like a bad or unworthy person, none of them agreed.

This is where the typical sex addiction recovery fails. At large, the therapy world assumes the negative feelings that lead to addiction come from feelings of worthlessness. Therapists tend to focus on the use of sex and porn as a coping mechanism used to avoid negative emotions and feelings of inadequacy.

However, in my experience working with high achievers, this does not appear to be the main cause of their compulsive sexual behavior.

They are not so much looking to avoid negative emotions as they are chasing positive ones. Rather than avoiding worthlessness or unworthiness, they are typically seeking respect and admiration, attention and validation from others. Their sexually compulsive behavior usually revolves around chasing a story of success. They want to be wanted, to be lusted after. For them, sex and pornography are less of a coping mechanism and more of a means to an end.

So, if high achievers make up a mere 2% of the population, do not feel like a bad or unworthy person, are not often using sex or pornography to avoid negative emotions, and connect best with other guys like them, can we agree they might need a recovery plan that looks different from the one established for 98% of the general population?

> To overcome sex and porn addiction, you must:
>
> 1) Discover what triggers your compulsivity and how to avoid it.
> 2) Get to the root cause of your sexually compulsive behavior.
> 3) Form deep connections with other sex addicts who understand and can support you.

If you find that the typical sex addiction treatment approaches are not working for you, speak up. If you have not found a group of men who you can relate to and enjoy recovering with, then find another group. This is your recovery, and it is on you to make it work.

You Are Not Powerless

Step one of the twelve steps states, "We admitted we were powerless over addictive sexual behavior."[3] If there's one

---

3 *Sex Addicts Anonymous. Sex Addicts Anonymous: 3rd Edition Conference Approved.* Houston: Sex Addicts Anonymous, 2017.

thing that will help you in your recovery, it's this: you are not powerless. You were not born with these behaviors. You used your power to create them—you are the only person who has the power to get rid of them.

It's important to note, there is a difference between powerlessness and surrender. Power is the ability to direct or influence behavior or the course of events. Surrender is the act of ceasing resistance to an enemy or opponent. In this case, the enemy or opponent is your compulsive sexual behavior.

You must surrender to the reality of your current situation in order to overcome your addiction. But don't give away your power.

If you are a high achiever, you know how powerful you can be once you set your mind to something. The question is, how do you position your sex addiction recovery so that you can put your mind to it?

It's a Process Addiction

Sex addiction is a new diagnosis. The term did not begin to be widely used until the mid-1980s. Even now (as I write this book), sex addiction is not an accepted diagnosis in the DSM-5, the official diagnostic tool of the American Psychiatric Association. There remains much to learn about sex addiction, which means treatment strategies are all over the map.

Sex addiction is a process addiction—the addict has become addicted to a thinking process. A process addiction is characterized by a lessening of control, persistent seeking, and significant harm even though no addictive substance is involved.[4]

Unlike a substance addiction, where the brain is affected by injecting, smoking, or ingesting an external substance, a process addiction uses thinking as the drug. If the thoughts are exciting, desirable, or validating, it is likely the person thinking these thoughts will find ways to entertain them again. In the case of the high achiever, the commonly pursued thoughts often have to do with being successful, superior, attractive, admired, desirable, respected, powerful, in control, special, or unique. In our society, engaging in romantic relationships, sex, and the garnering of feedback related to one's sex appeal will activate many of these brain processes, resulting in feelings of fulfillment, superiority, and success. High achievers long for these feelings, thus making them potentially addictive.

---

4 Daniel Kardefelt-Winther, Alexandre Heeren, Andriano Schimmernti, et al., "How can we conceptualize behavioural addiction without pathologizing common behaviours," *Addiction 112, No. 10* (2017): 1709-1715, https://doi.org/10.1111/add.13763.

Let's say you are sitting at a hotel lobby bar. You look over to see a woman expressing an interest in you. Your brain may be thinking, "She finds me attractive; she definitely wants to sleep with me; out of all the guys here, she is choosing me; I must be the most desirable man in the room."

If your brain enjoys these thoughts, you will probably feel desired, superior, wanted, and lusted after. The better they make you feel, the more likely you are to seek them out again. If these feelings are rare, you may be more compelled to repeat this behavior. If you prefer these feelings to the ones you experience on a regular basis, there is the potential to become reliant on them. Thus begins a process addiction.

So, the term process addiction is actually more accurate than sex addiction. "Well, that's just semantics," you may say. But using the wrong term can do more harm than good. When the focus is on being a sex addict, it's all about not doing sexual things, versus changing the way you think. Instead of looking for the root cause of your behavior, you spend your time trying to stop the side effects. The word "sex addict" is especially harmful for your wife. Afterall, who wants to be married to a sex, porn, or love addict?

Now, I'm not saying that sex addiction is not a real thing. It most certainly is. My story is one of many.

One of the men at one of my first intensives was in the same boat. He had been faithful and sexually sober for almost two years. He was at a coffee shop working on his laptop when he locked eyes with a beautiful woman sitting at the table across from him. He enjoyed her attention as she enjoyed his. After exchanging looks for nearly an hour, she walked over to him and gave him her phone number. With the last hour spent in lust, imagining all the things he would like to do to her in bed, he decided to send her a text message just a few hours later. This relationship would quickly turn physical. Hence, the reason he was at another sex addiction treatment intensive. But this time his wife asked him to move out and sign a one-year lease on his own apartment. Yes, he was sexually sober for two years, but his process addiction was alive and well.

Every process addiction is unique to the addict. For some, it's about power and control. For others, it's about being wanted and lusted after, or avoiding boredom and escaping reality. For many, it's about superiority and feeling better than others. Rather than being addicted to sex, they are addicted to stories or fantasies that make them believe they are who they want to be. Any behavior that validates that notion, is a behavior they will likely repeat.

There are many behaviors that can activate the same processes. The most common is the addiction to money, success, and achievement. Workaholism is socially accepted and often rewarded. Therefore, you do not often see men doing anything to break that addiction.

Another common process addiction we see in high achievers involves the lethal combination of people pleasing, attention seeking, and the compulsion to impress others. Outside of work, their attention focuses on ways to standout and be impressive. It may be buying clothes, shoes, watches, or cars that enhance their status. It could also be placing themselves in social situations where they are able to charm and seduce others into thinking they are rare, exceptional, or unusually great. Most people enjoy being admired and appreciated, but becoming addicted to these behaviors will leave you feeling unhappy or unfulfilled without that attention and affirmation.

> Process addiction is not like substance addiction; simply stopping porn and sex will not be enough to make you sober. Unless you change the brain process, you may still be an addict.

Understand What You're Recovering From

When your marriage is about to end, it's normal to want to dive deep into your recovery to prove to your wife that you are willing to do anything to change. If you're in the beginning of the traditional recovery process, this often means going to 12-step meetings or checking into a residential rehab facility for sex addiction.

These treatment programs are designed to help someone who has become chemically dependent on sex, porn, or affairs. All men are forced into this one treatment avenue because sex addiction is the most commonly used term to describe unwanted sexual behavior,

However, if your compulsive sexual behaviours stem from a desire for attention and validation, from an overwhelming need for control, and from a maladaptive attempt to fulfill your unmet human needs, you will not achieve long-term sobriety with such strategies. Not because they don't work, but because you're being treated for a condition that does not address the main reason why you engage in this behavior.

You must know what, exactly, you are recovering from. You must address each component that has created your unwanted sexual behaviors and relieve them with the appropriate strategies.

For most high achievers, it's prioritizing success over everything else. If that's you, your desire to be successful will overtake your desire to have a deeply connected relationship with your wife. That obsession with success—getting attention, earning respect—is your primary addiction, not sex. Therefore, your treatment approach should focus on these thought processes instead of a chemically dependent sex or porn addiction.

Enthusiasm is great, but it won't do a whole lot of good if it's focused in the wrong direction. You cannot go all-in on your recovery until you know what it is you need to recover from. To start, you need to determine what drives your compulsive sexual behavior. This clarity will give you a blueprint of your unique process addiction. From there, you can make the necessary changes to counter your processes addiction.

3

How To Beat This Addiction

The term sex addiction is controversial in the world of psychology. According to many professionals, not all sex addicts are actually addicted to sex. Some are chasing something else. These men are diagnosed as having compulsive sexual behavior.

Similar to sex addiction, those with compulsive sexual behavior are unable to stop despite the negative consequences. However, they are not necessarily "addicted."

They tend to be a particular type of man, as well: high achievers, executives, business and sales professionals, lawyers, doctors, professional athletes, and entrepreneurs. They are men who continue to struggle with urges and desires that threaten their marriage. Either the 12-step programs do not work for them, or they lack in-person groups nearby, leaving them vulnerable to setbacks. These men know that they need connection to overcome this addiction but find it difficult to relate to those who do not face the struggles unique to their level of success.

That's why Certified Sex Addition Therapists often refer them to my program, *The Successful Addict*; there they can find a deeply connected recovery group that operates like a high-level mastermind.

Much like we do in these recovery groups, we're going to take some time to focus on four categories of compulsive sexual behavior. This will help you uncover the nub of the issue: process addiction. You must examine the very thought processes that lead to unwanted sexual behavior and compulsions, or you will remain vulnerable to setbacks and associated consequences, including a failed marriage.

Category 1: Addiction

The addictive component of compulsive sexual behavior is the chemical dependency on sex, porn, or affairs. This is the primary focus of most sex addiction literature and treatment. Sex addicts report a nagging or buzzing, a pull or persistent urge that feels positively chemical. For someone who has never confronted addiction, this feeling is hard to comprehend. But for the addict, in that moment, they believe the only way to make that unpleasant feeling go away is to cave into their addiction. Yes, in a sober world, there are other options besides sex and porn. However, for the addict, it truly feels like there is no other choice but to act out sexually.

Engaging in the unwanted sexual behavior is what sex addicts refer to as "acting out." In recovery groups, you will often hear addicts say, "I acted out." When they say this, it means that they violated their sexual sobriety.

The addictive component of compulsive sexual behavior comes from a dependency on unwanted sexual behavior. It typically starts off innocently enough. Curiosity or sexual exploration usually drives a person to watch porn, masturbate, or have sex for the first time. Because sex is enjoyable, this curiosity often evolves into an intentional practice with the goal of seeking pleasure. In the healthy person, sexual pleasure is used in moderation. The addiction starts when the sexual behavior is used as a coping mechanism. The behavior is no longer innocent, it has traversed a line into "acting out." Coping mechanisms of any kind help us avoid unpleasant emotions; they shift our attention away from something to which we do not want to pay attention.

Addiction is often perceived as a problem for pleasure seekers. This is not the case. Dopamine is known as the addictive neurotransmitter. The belief that addicts seek dopamine for the pleasure it provides was disproven in 1989 by a famous study by Berridge, Venier, and Robinson.[5] They found dopamine did not provide pleasure; rather, it's responsible for focus and motivation. Our bodies produce dopamine in anticipation of the reward, not by the reward itself.

Addicts have learned that any behavior that releases dopamine will shift their attention towards the activity releasing the dopamine. This is perfect for those who want to avoid feeling unpleasant emotions or avoid thinking about something they don't want to think about. In both cases, the addict uses dopamine to cope with boredom, stress, or pain—to escape their life situation.

Sex, porn, and affairs can provide huge dopamine hits. It covers up negative feelings, it's easier to hide from others, and can be efficiently worked into one's schedule. It's why high achievers often gravitate towards sex as opposed to other drugs. Yet, like all addictions, the associated high of engaging in this behavior wears off

5 Bhav Neurosci, "Taste reactivity analysis of 6-hydroxydopamine-induced aphagia: implications for arousal and anhedonia hypotheses of dopamine function," *National Library of Medicine* (1989), https://pubmed.ncbi.nlm.nih.gov/2493791.

more quickly; before long, it requires progressive "use" to provide the same desired level of dopamine. This is why most sex addicts end up seeking wider varieties of pornography and end up engaging in riskier sexual activity. (We will dive further into sex addiction and what addicts need to do to recover in later chapters.)

The field of sex addiction tends to treat every guy as if he is using sex as a coping mechanism. It is assumed that he is "addicted." However, most high achievers can go months in between acting out behaviours. Therefore, calling them a sex addict is totally inaccurate. Even worse, using addiction treatment strategies will end up proving to be ineffective. If you do not believe that you are chemically addicted to sex and pornography, make sure that you are examining other aspects of compulsive behavior to ensure that you are actually going to get better.

Category 2: Societal and Masculine Norms

While not as commonly discussed in the literature and treatment programs, it is my belief that societal and masculine norms are one of the biggest contributors to why high-achieving men engage in compulsive sexual behaviors.

High achievers are hyperaware of what other people find impressive. After all, to truly be considered such, you need to know what people consider "difficult to achieve." This hyperawareness of others is a superpower.

In a study on successful people, Dr. Martin Kilduff, Professor of Organizational Behavior at the University of Cambridge, found high achievers move into central positions within social networks and enjoy early promotions in their careers. According to Dr. Kilduff, their ability to act as social chameleons allows them to emerge as leaders because they are "constantly acting, putting on impressions, worrying about the front-stage, back-stage; it's about staging performances, being in the public eye, socially constructing [their] persona."[6] Their ability to impress others is largely responsible for their financial success.

On the flip side, their desire to impress the masses leaves them highly susceptible to society's norms and influences . . .

Society has normalized the use of sex for profit and pleasure. One in four internet searches are pornographic in nature.[7] Strip clubs and escort services are easily acces-

---

6 Knowledge@SMU, "High Self-Monitors: A Chameleon, a Magnet, a Leader," *Institutional Knowledge at Singapore Management University* (2019), https://ink.library.smu.edu.sg/ksmu/264.

7 Webroot. "Internet Pornography by the Numbers." Webroot Resources. n.d. Accessed January 7, 2025. https://www.webroot.com/us/en/resources/tips-articles/internet-pornography-by-the-numbers#

sible and legally practiced in cities across the country. New social media websites allow ordinary women to create a profile and charge men for sexually explicit images. Large corporations use the female body as a marketing tool to sell everything from beer to fast cars.

Society defines what is "normal." As these practices become more mainstream, a new normal is being redefined with each passing day. But what if it shouldn't be normal? What if it's harming people? What if it's encouraging the capacity to destroy the relationships that matter most, namely the ones you have with yourself, your wife, and your family?

It's easy to minimize or justify things when everyone is doing it. But this does not mean that it is not causing harm. It does not mean that your wife will feel valued, cared for, or included in your priorities.

The same goes for masculine norms. These begin early in life when boys are trying to figure out what it means to be a man. One of the best examples of early masculine normalization is when a kid finds his father's porn collection. Most people focus on how traumatizing it is for a twelve-year-old boy to unexpectedly stumble across pornographic images. Yes, this is traumatic. However, the fact that the father hid the porn in the first place, causes far more harm. It sends a very clear message: men look at naked women even when they are married, and they need to hide it.

This message is further exacerbated if the boy discovers his mom knows about the pornography collection and has accepted it. Then, the message becomes: men look at naked women and your wife must learn to be okay with it. Most men have experienced something similar early on in their life, where it was accepted as a normal masculine practice to view pornography. Accepting this as normal at such an early age sets them up for further objectification of women in the future.

From early puberty, boys start talking about women like objects to be conquered. This ideology typically continues through college. Sleeping with as many attractive women as possible is often seen as a sign of accomplishment. In many male circles, it is common to seduce women at bars even when they are married. Work trips and conferences are often seen as an opportunity to take a break from marriage and enjoy a few days as a bachelor. Men will often cover for their friends and colleagues to ensure their wives do not discover what is going on, making this behavior systemic.

How do you know if societal or masculine norms are contributing to your compulsivity? If you no longer feel guilt when you engage in unwanted sexual behaviors. This is the problem with society normalizing porn, strip clubs, chat sites, massage parlours, and other forms of casual sex. Once enough people consider a behavior "normal," it alters your moral compass; it removes the guilt you used to feel when acting out of your value system.

Category 3: Control and Deception

For some, lying feels good. Deceiving someone and getting away with it gives a sense of power and control. But some like lying more than others. Boys who grow up in a strict or highly structured household, for instance, learn early on that lying gives them a "one-up" over their parents, friends, and other adults. They enjoy this one-up feeling, so they lie again and again. By the time they are teenagers, their lying has become automatic.

Many of the men in my recovery groups are also good liars. In their sobriety, they will not look at porn or engage in sexual behavior. Yet they have this strange urge to keep their deceptive sexuality alive. They'll look for prostitutes with no intention of hiring them, and surf non-pornographic websites or apps to see if they can find something "forbidden." The motive is not to view porn; if they really wanted to, they could find a way. The motive is to perpetuate the deception.

This type of behavior is still acting out; it's part of process addiction. It wants to keep secretive sexual behavior hidden; it's the internal voice that says, "My sexuality is my business, and I should be able to do it if I want to."

Men often wonder why they lie. For some, it's simply a way to avoid shame, judgement, and divorce. It can also be a desire for control. Men who like control enjoy having a secret sexual life. For them, it's not about the sex, porn, or affairs; it's about the feeling of keeping a secret. It provides them with a sense of independence and control. For these men, recovery can be challenging. As their sexual behavior is put under the microscope, they begin having more urges to act out. The more their behavior is monitored and policed, the more their addict brain wants to do what they are not allowed to do. For the person who desires control, taking away their sense of privacy can often increase their desire to do the very things they are trying not to do.

Even in recovery, the compulsion remains. The more loved ones "spy" on them, the more they want to do the things they're trying to prevent; the more controls are applied to electronic devices, the more they want to rebel and find ways around the restrictions. In such cases, the very restrictions intended to help them stay sober, serve as a detriment; without rules, blockers, and restrictions, there's nothing left to rebel against.

How do you know if control and deception are contributing to your compulsive sexual behavior? If you no longer value integrity. People who value integrity don't lie. They never bend the rules or compromise their values. If you want to control how you are perceived more than you value your integrity, you will lie to protect your agenda.

Category 4: Using Sex to Meet Your Human Needs

Abraham Maslow was an American psychologist most famous for his hierarchy of human needs. Maslow discovered that humans all have the same five basic needs: survival, safety, connection, self-esteem, and self-actualization.[8]

We're hardwired at birth to fulfill these needs. The problem is that nobody teaches us how to get these needs met. Throughout life, we each learn through observation and experience how to get what we need from others and the environment. There's a lot of guesswork. Through

---

8 Saul McLeod, "Maslow's Hierarchy of Needs," Simply Psychology (2024), https://www.simplypsychology.org/maslow.html.

trial and error, we eventually find a way to meet our needs, while giving our best effort at living a fulfilling existence. As you can imagine, sex and sex appeal end up working their way into our plans.

Sex tends to feed two of the five human needs: connection and esteem. We each need to connect with others and form meaningful relationships. Unfortunately, we often mistake sex and attraction for connection, since it happens between two people. In reality, you can have sex and be attracted to someone without connecting with them.

When men do not feel enough connection, they may seek sex or relationships outside of their marriage. Typically, sex and affairs do not fulfill what they are after—because true connection is about intimacy not sex. Dan Drake, expert in intimacy after sexual betrayal, determined that connection only happens when the relationship has honesty, safety, trust, and vulnerability. Yes, sex can enhance the connection between two people. But only when the relationship has all the elements required for true intimacy.[9]

Connection and belonging are about a sense of inclusion and togetherness. Humans need to feel they belong

9 "The Intimacy Pyramid: Creating Connections That Stand the Test of Time," The Intimacy Pyramid, accessed November 11, 2024, https://intimacypyramid.com.

to a group of people and that those people want them around. High achievers are often torn between two forms of connection: they crave human connection, just like everyone else—love, intimacy, friends, and family; yet they also want to belong to a social status that will help them make an impact.

Social status has been around for centuries, and it often dictates a person's ability to interact and influence others. Super successful people tend to have a natural pull towards a particular social status. It's as if their body knows that they need to belong to this group to carry out their life's purpose. In most cases, they are not wrong.

Another big need is esteem—the need to feel respected, admired, and appreciated. High achievers view life as a contest that needs to be won. That means there are winners and there are losers, which is where they begin to develop their superiority complex. They believe those at "the top" are winning the game and are better than others. This feeling of superiority is often confused with respect and admiration. But superior is a subjective measure. You can believe that you are "superior" and still not feel respect and admiration from your peers.

Respect is not about sex and money. It's about doing the hard things that others are not brave enough to do. Admiration is not about having a six-pack. It's about spending your time doing things that make a difference and living a life bigger than yourself.

Sex and lust have mistakenly been clumped in with esteem. In successful male culture, being lusted after is one of the biggest compliments: the more women want you, the more admired and respected you must be. It sounds ridiculous. But this belief is perpetuated on TV and in the movies. So, it makes sense that boys learn this at a young age and never stop to question its validity.

Here are the most common false beliefs regarding esteem that prevent sex addicts from recovering:

1) The more I accomplish, the more valuable I am.

2) Women are more attracted to financially successful men.

3) The more money I have, the more people will admire me.

4) My wife's attention alone is not enough to make me feel wanted and desired.

5) I feel better when I know that women find me attractive and want to have sex with me. The more women who do, the more desirable I know that I am.

For each of these false beliefs, there are hundreds more like them. But it's important to remember they are false ("not in accordance with truth") beliefs ("trust, faith, or confidence in something"). Every man who has ever thought these believed them to be true at one point or another.

The key is to consider the opposing belief; for example:

1) Is it possible that people admire those who accomplish challenging things regardless of how much money is made?

2) What if women are attracted to men with a strong sense of self and a clear direction?

3) What if being desired for your financial success or your appearance is always unfulfilling? What if true fulfillment comes when they choose you based on your unique abilities?

4) Is it possible that the number of women who want to sleep with you has nothing to do with living a fulfilling life?

Using women and sex to meet a basic human need is something learned by watching others. Many men have felt the lack of love, connection, belonging, respect, and admiration. They believed sex or affairs were going to resolve these unmet needs. They believed a fantasy. What's not seen is the emptiness felt each night when they are left with an even deeper hole waiting to be filled.

How do you know if you are using sex to satisfy your unmet human needs? If you feel extremely justified in your desire to act out sexually. When human needs are unmet, you will feel a strong biological desire to meet them. You will feel as if you need attention, validation, sex, or physical touch.

But there's a difference between your biological human needs and your perception of how they are met. Your need for connection and esteem is far more complex and will require more than sex to get them met.

Bigger Than You Think

These four components of compulsive sexuality show how this problem is much bigger than addiction. When it comes to sex and porn, there are many factors at play that can contribute to your compulsivity. This is not to intimidate or overwhelm you. It's to give you a solid appreciation for the scope of the problem.

According to research performed by Jennifer Schneider MD, among men with more than five years in recovery, 64.3% reported having relapsed.[10] This means after five years, only 35.7% of men achieved recovery without relapse. I believe this recovery rate is not low because sex addiction recovery is hard; it's low because most men are not examining all four components of their compulsive behavior.

Remember, sex addiction is a process addiction. If you want to achieve a full recovery, you need to examine all the thought processes that play into your compulsive sexual behavior. It can be very challenging to examine these four elements on your own as the thoughts have become so automatic you hardly notice them. This is why recovery groups are considered the most effective treatment strategy for sex addicts. You will learn more watching other men navigate their own process addiction than you will trying to dive into your addiction on your own. While every addict's brain processes are unique to them, hearing their stories will often shine light on your own process addiction.

At our sex addiction retreats, we use a formula that allows each person to present their process addiction to the other men in the group. This enlightening process is a

10 Jennifer P. Schneider, "Editorial: Sex Addition and the Family," *Sexual Addition & Compulsivity* 3, No. 2 (1996): https://doi.org/10.1080/10720169608400102.

relatively new strategy called co-learning, which allows a group of like-minded people to solve a common problem. Men who participate in these retreats often report that they learned more in four days than in years of therapy.

Those thoughts and beliefs you previously considered "normal," conflict with the life you have been trying to create. Once you see the insanity of your behavior, that living this way will leave you empty and alone, you can finally make the changes you have been working so hard to make.

Addiction is Human

Humans want things. It's what we do and how we are designed for survival. We want to do more of what makes us feel good and less of what makes us feel bad. Developing a sex addiction doesn't make you weird. You could have very easily chosen bingeing TV shows, alcohol, drugs, shopping, gossip, spending hours on social media, or playing video games. But you didn't. You chose porn, sex, affairs, emotional affairs, or one of the many combinations.

It is important to understand that sex addiction doesn't make you a pervert. On the contrary, our society makes it very easy to objectify women. Pornography and masturbation are some of the first forms of intense pleasure boys discover when they are young.

Not to downplay or belittle sex addiction. As a recovering sex addict, I can tell you that this addiction is one of the worst I have seen. But it's important that you know you are not alone and there's nothing wrong with you.

You are not a freak. I work with men who are wildly successful in sales and business. I've worked with doctors, lawyers, dentists, orthodontists, professional athletes, celebrities, sales professionals, and all sorts of entrepreneurs. Many of them are high achievers worth millions of dollars. They have worked tirelessly striving to be the best at what they do. Yet, despite all their efforts to build the perfect life, they struggle with a sex addiction that has the potential to ruin everything.

Sex addiction tends to sneak up on people. Despite knowing that their behavior is inappropriate, most sex addicts fail to recognize that their behaviour is compulsive. Because sex is a biological need, men often think there's nothing they can do about their sexual desires. It isn't until their wife discovers them, and they begin their recovery work, that they finally realize their compulsive sexual behaviors are not biologically driven. You weren't born with these fantasies and desires. You learned them.

And just as you learned them, you can unlearn them if you want to.

In the beginning, you may not feel like you are an addict or compulsive (I certainly didn't). In our society, an addict is often portrayed as a degenerate who can barely get out of bed in the morning. The truth is many addicts know how to feed their addiction without disrupting their lives. You have probably heard this phase called denial. It's the unconscious refusal to acknowledge the reality of your situation. Denial is a defense mechanism used by addicts to shield themselves from guilt, maintain control, and avoid making a difficult change. It is not that the addict is denying they are an addict. They honestly have no idea that they are addicted.

Addiction isn't about being consumed by sex or porn. Here's the definition we will use, "engaging in behaviors that you cannot stop doing even though you know it makes you less of the man you want to be." If your sexual behavior has led you to read this book, this definition probably describes you.

Sex Addiction Is Alienating

When an alcoholic or a drug addict hits rock bottom, they are often shown grace and compassion. Post about substance addiction on social media and it's likely met with supportive comments, with people reaching out to offer encouragement, friends and family members stepping up to help where they can.

This is not the case for sex addicts. As our culture currently stands, sex is a private matter that carries with it judgement and shame. Sex is very personal and plays a significant role in marriage and relationships. For these reasons, sex addicts are rarely shown compassion or grace, especially from their spouses.

Addicts are at their lowest of lows when they hit rock bottom. They are experiencing the worst aspects of shame, guilt, and humiliation. This is when they need support and compassion the most. For sex addicts, support is hard to come by. Not only can they not reach out for help from their community, they are also unable to rely on their primary attachment figure, their wife. Which makes this addiction very isolating.

For your wife, sexual betrayal has flipped her world upside down. Her husband, the one whom she has given herself to and trusted as her partner for life, has chosen other women over her. If the love of her life could do this to her, how can she trust anyone ever again?

While never your intent, your actions have traumatized your wife in ways that will damage her nervous system. Michelle Mays, one of the leading experts in betrayal recovery, calls sexual betrayal a "survival-level threat."[11] After betrayal, your wife will operate in a world where she is unable to trust anyone, including herself. You made her feel unattractive, undesired, and easily replaceable. You destroyed her past, her present, and everything she was hoping life would be. Unlike other addictions, the wives of sex addicts are the ones who get the worst of it. Due to the unique nature of this type of betrayal, they often lack support and understanding from friends, parents, and even some therapists. Their recovery is oftentimes far worse than that of the addict as they must heal multiple areas of their lives.

Sexual betrayal is the ugliest part of this addiction. As a sex addict, it can be hard to live with the reality of what you have done to your wife. This is unfortunate, as shame is the number one thing that will prevent a sex addict from healing. It is hard enough to deal with an addiction; it is even harder when you must show up for your wife in a way you have never shown up before. To heal, she will need full transparency, empathy, and deep connection—all which are difficult for sex addicts to tap into. That's because sex addition is an intimacy disorder (according

11 Michelle Mays, *The Betrayal Bind: How to Heal When the Person You Love the Most Has Hurt You the Worst* (Tantor Audio, 2023), Kindle.

to Dr. Michael Barta).[12] And that makes empathy, vulnerability, and honesty difficult for sex addicts to express.

While it seems impossible at times, healing your marriage after sexual betrayal is possible.

> If you are looking for ways to accelerate the healing of your marriage, I have developed a checklist that can help you assemble everything you need. You'll find it at **successfuladdict.com/ savemymarriage**

Sex Addiction Is Hard to Stop

Sex addiction is incredibly hard to stop. It is estimated that only 36% of men with sex addiction can achieve long-term sobriety without significant relapse.[13] Even if you're able to stop acting out, lustful thoughts, objectification of women, and fantasy often persist for years into sobriety. It's a big part of our culture and hard to completely

---

12 Michael Barta, *TINSA: A Neurological Approach to the Treatment of Sex Addiction* (Michael, 2020), Kindle.

13 Jennifer P. Schneider, M. Deborah Corley, Richard K. Irons, "Surviving Disclosure of Infidelity: Results of an International Survey of 164 Recovering Sex Addicts and Partners," *Sexual Addiction & Compulsivity* 5, No. 3 (1998): 189-218, https://doi.org/10.1080/10720169808400162.

escape it. But this is not what makes sex addiction so difficult to overcome ...

One, sex is a biological desire necessary to sustain life. Humans need to have sex to repopulate the earth. Because sex addiction is linked so closely to man's drive to survive, it makes recovery much more challenging.

Two (as we touched on previously), sex addiction is a result of a thought process. Because the thought processes are different for each addict, there is no one size fits all treatment program for sex and porn addicts. The unique presentation of each sex addiction is the reason that it is so complex to treat. Not because it is more addicting than other addictions, but because the thought processes are unique to each addict.

Imagine if every car we drove was custom-built and one of a kind. If you took it to the repair shop and the mechanic had never seen one like it before, it would take more time to diagnose the problem, even more time to figure out how to repair it. This is what it's like for sex addicts. Your addiction is unique to you and one of a kind. Therefore, it will require a unique treatment strategy to discover what made you this way and what you need to do to stop it.

4

Does Your Past Matter?

A s a high achiever focused on moving forward, you may believe the past does not matter. You may have also believed that you would never get to this point. *Why would someone do such things? How could I have let this happen?* The answer is in your past. Life experiences leading up to this point provided a worldview that allowed these things. You developed a series of beliefs that justified acting out sexually with zero consideration of others. These beliefs allowed secrecy, lying, casual sex, and viewing pornography to enter your life without setting off internal alarms.

In this delusional world, you may have experienced (and therefore) believe:

- Enjoying naked women is normal and getting married doesn't change that.
- Getting attention from women is a normal desire and you can be married and still enjoy it.
- Sex is a human need; monogamy is unnatural.
- Life is meant to be enjoyed—as long as it is consensual, what's the big deal?
- Women don't understand what it's like to be a guy.
- If sex workers and porn stars didn't like it, why would they do it?
- It's not cheating if it's just porn.

Chances are good you always knew what you were doing is wrong—it violates your values and core beliefs. That's why you hid it. The question is, where did this worldview come from? Well, let's take a look back . . .

Ages Zero to Twelve

Ages zero to twelve are the most formative years of your life.[14] When you are born, you have no understanding of

---

14 "Early Childhood Development," UNICEF, accessed September 16, 2024, https://data.unicef.org/topic/early-childhood-development/overview/.

how the world works. You have no references as to how to make sense of what is going on around you. Good and bad, right and wrong, better or worse—all of these concepts are formed between the ages of zero and twelve. But what happens when the people around you are not modeling a healthy way of living life? What if your early life experiences do not reflect how the world actually works?

Even as a child, you are hardwired to meet your human needs. Like adults, children are always thinking about how they are going to meet their needs for connection, love, belonging, respect, and admiration.

Early life experiences shape your view of yourself and your view of the world—as a fully developed adult, you are likely still using old beliefs established during those formative years in an effort to meet your needs. To change those beliefs, you first need to discover why you started believing them in the first place.

I suggest examining the years up to age twelve. Before the age of twelve, your beliefs are still forming. This is why many children are sexually molested without knowing what happened to them. If the perpetrator tells them that this behavior is "normal," the child is likely to believe them. It's not until they are adults that they realize this interaction is inappropriate. But how damaging was that experience; what impact did that sexual encounter have on their view of sex as an adult?

When you look back to those first twelve years of your life, there are experiences that shaped you significantly. Recovering from your sex addiction will require you to look at as many of those experiences as you possibly can and mine them for the beliefs you took away from them. Mind you, at times it's the small ones that create the most suffering later in life.

Maybe your girlfriend broke up with you for another boy in class. You might conclude that if only you were more athletic, muscular, or better dressed, she would have stayed with you. This seemingly small breakup might cause you to chase money and enhance your appearance as an adult.

Maybe your family dog died when you were young. You cried at school the next day, thinking about the loss of your beloved pet, and the other boys made fun of you for crying. You might conclude that showing your emotions in public is a sign of weakness. As an adult you might choose to hide your sadness from other men out of fear of being judged or ridiculed.

Maybe your father never expressed his emotions; your mother was the only one in the house who showed signs of sadness or frustration. You might conclude that women are the only ones allowed to express their feelings publicly. As an adult, you might hide your feelings as a symbol of your masculinity.

Maybe you experienced a falling out with a friend; as a result, a few of your closest friends (all from wealthier families than yours) stopped inviting you to hang out with them. You might conclude that they would have continued to have you around if your family had more money. From that day forward, you made plans to never be poor again.

Maybe your childhood experiences include being bullied for a pair of shoes you wore to school. You might conclude that people judge others based on how they look. If you were bullied again for a similar reason, you may conclude that your appearance will dictate your ability to fit in socially. As an adult, your outward appearance may become a massive focus.

Finding the experiences and their associated memories that shaped your sex addiction most can be challenging to do on your own. This is why creating an inventory of formative experiences is one of the first things we do at my in-person sex addiction retreats. Listening to the other men in the group allows you to remember more and more about your life and what it was like to be you in those first twelve years. This exercise leads to some of the biggest breakthroughs, as it's those early beliefs that affect us the most.

It may seem ridiculous that one event can alter your life forever. But this is what humans do, and it can have a profound impact on what you choose (and choose not) to do.

Normal Is Not Normal

Children grow up believing what they see and hear. If they see everyone around them worried about the future and striving to be more, get more, and have more, they will grow up believing that is the way life is supposed to be. The result is a child who grows up to be like everyone else: under constant pressure to get better looking, make more money, and accomplish as many things as possible.

Normal is not normal. Normal is what people make it. If the people around you believe that life is a contest that needs to be won, then most people will be living their lives trying to win that contest.

Normal doesn't mean it's right; it simply means it's what most people are doing. So, what happens if most people are wrong? Look around . . .

We live in the most depressed and unsatisfied society that has ever existed. Most people believe that you are born inadequate and that you need to spend your entire life proving your value. In this world, some people never prove their value. They end up stuck in the same job, doing work they despise.

It's terrifying to think of becoming one of those people. So, we wake up every day looking for ways to become more valuable. But the conclusion at the end of each day is the same, "I wish I had done more today."

Addiction is on the rise. According to a study by California State University, 10% of Americans, or 33.19 million people, are addicted to social media. In a 2021 evaluation by the World Health Organization found that 3.05% of the world population, or around 60 million people, currently have a video gaming disorder.[15] And the same goes for sex and porn addiction. A study published in the JAMA Network found that 10.3% of men and 7% of women in the United Stated have compulsive sexual behavior disorder. This study was published in 2018, and

---

15 Matthew Wr Stevens, Diana Dorstyn, Daniel L King, et al, "Global Prevalence of Gaming Disorder: A Systematic Review and Meta-Analysis," *Australian & New Zealand Journal of Psychiatry* 55, no. 6 (2020): 928, https://doi.org/10.1177/0004867420962851.

it is estimated that number has increased significantly in both men and women.[16]

Here's my theory: For centuries, our ancestors have been making the world easier and easier for us to live in. Inventions like the car, dishwasher, and smartphone were intended to give us our time back so that we could spend more time doing things that make a difference. Instead, we have more time to sit with our feelings of inadequacy and lack of achievement.

> Rather than using our newfound free time to find something to fix, we waste it looking for ways to stop the negative feelings. This increases the likelihood of becoming an addict.

Ages Twelve to Twenty-Five

Younger years may be the most formative, but what you learn about life between ages twelve and twenty-five plays an extremely significant role—especially when it

---

16 Janna A. Dickensen, Neil Gleason, Eli Coleman, et al, "Prevalence of Distress Associated with Difficulty Controlling Sexual Urges, Feelings, and Behaviors in the United States," JAMA Network 1, no. 7 (2018), doi:10.1001/jamanetworkopen.2018.4468.

comes to your addiction. The transactional analysis theory labels this phase of your life "the adapted child."[17]

The adapted child is the second iteration of your belief system. These adaptations are based on what you initially came to believe about yourself and the world around you. Beliefs up to the age of twelve set the stage for how challenging you think it will be to get your needs met; beliefs formed between the age of twelve and twenty-five dictate what you are going to do about it.

Before twelve years of age, you are primarily an observer of the life around you. You take in information and think about what it all means. After age twelve, you begin taking more action to meet your needs and become the person you want to be. It's between twelve and twenty-five that men may begin researching things online, working out, reading books, asking more questions, and taking more chances. This phase of life is more about cause and effect. *When I do something, what happens as a result of my actions?*

Then you extrapolate. You apply the lessons you learned from your actions and apply it to everything

---

17 Sezgin Bekir and Ergyul Tair, "Functional Ego States, Behavior Patterns, and Social Interaction of Bulgarian Adolescents and Their Parents," *Societies* 13, No. 7 (2023): 154, https://doi.org/10.3390/soc13070154.

else in life that appears similar. When you fail or get an unwanted result in one area, everything that even resembles that area begins to look riskier. If you are rejected on your first attempt at asking a girl out, you become much less likely to make another attempt until you have done everything you can to prevent another rejection.

Think of it this way: The beliefs you formed before the age of twelve dictate the way you think the world works. The beliefs you formed after the age of twelve dictate the rules of that world, and how you can become successful. When the rules conflict with your values, your desire for success convinces you to compromise those values. Before you know it, you're behaving in ways you said you never would.

Here's an example: In middle school, a boy lands the girl of his dreams. She's confident, pretty, and outgoing—the very things he is not. She is his first girlfriend. They hold hands at football games, and she puts her head on his shoulder at the movies. He's experiencing very strong feelings for a thirteen-year-old. Then, a few weeks later, he walks into school after getting off the bus, and is greeted by one of his friends boasting that he flirted with his girlfriend in the hot tub at a party over the weekend, a party to which he was not invited.

Imagine that sinking heart. There's embarrassment, betrayal, exclusion. Even if the boy pretends not to care, you know he's never felt more insignificant. Suddenly, he starts to believe certain things. When the girl breaks up with him a week later, he forms even more beliefs about the world around him. Some of those beliefs spur action, to facilitate getting what he wants most:

- I need to get better if I want girls to like me back.

- I need nicer clothes.

- My parents are too poor and that is preventing me from making friends.

- I'm not confident enough or popular enough.

- I need to find a way to get into the "in" crowd.

Are those beliefs real? Depends on your definition of reality. To that boy, they feel extremely real—like facts of life. If he continues to believe them, they could lead to all sorts of problems in relationships, self-esteem, and how he treats others.

The beliefs formed between the ages of twelve and twenty-five stick with you. They can also derail your life significantly. Certain life experiences can alter your view of the world, causing you to do things in reaction to the past rather than what is actually going on in the present.

That's why so many men in the world today are reacting like little boys rather than healthy adults. Your past matters and it's likely the reason for most of your suffering today. That's why it's important for your recovery to eliminate beliefs that aren't true and to replace them with beliefs that are.

5

Why High Achievers Struggle with Compulsive Sexual Behavior

So, you've learned the ins and outs of compulsive sexual behavior, how your formative years played a part, that your path to recovery will be as unique as you are—and that you'll need to face each thought process that got you to this point. But there's one more thing you need to be aware of . . . something that, until this point, has been nothing but a positive. Mainly, it's the fact that you're a high achiever. High achieving males are a breed of their own, and that will present unique challenges in your struggle with sexually compulsive behavior.

Successful Male Culture

The message has been clear for the past 100 years: If you are a male and want to be successful, you need to make a lot of money, have a nice body, sleep with attractive women, and own a lot of fancy things. If you want to be somebody important, you need to accumulate as many of these things as you can. You'll find this message in books, on TV, in the movies, in advertising, and at social gatherings.

Take James Bond. He's the perfect guy. Women want him and men want to be him. He drives nice cars, spends lots of money, and travels the world. In each story, he uses his charisma to sleep with multiple beautiful women. It's easy to see how young boys might believe if only they were like him, they'd have the admiration of the whole world.

There are hundreds of thousands of males just like Bond who use their wealth, good looks, and power to live a seemingly magnificent life in books and on the screen—from the superhero who kicks ass all day and makes love to women all night, to the billionaire with an intimacy disorder who sexualizes women.

The pull is understandable. Belonging is a human need. So is esteem and recognition. Marketers understand these needs and use them to their advantage; they use wealth shaming and comparison as a marketing tool to prey on men's insecurities. If you don't buy what they're selling, you are somehow inadequate. This constant reminder of inadequacy is toxic to mental health. As a sex addict, these daily reminders pour gasoline on the feelings of being behind and not yet enough. Again, this makes addiction much worse.

Of course, the publishing, film, and marketing industries are not the only ones to blame. Regular men have normalized the image of "the successful man." Every man who is striving to get more money, have a better body, and sleep with more attractive women is to blame. As long as men normalize spending their time chasing these things, other men will continue wanting to do the same.

I am in no way judging any of these behaviors. There's nothing wrong with building wealth, maintaining great physical health, and making sure you are still attractive. However, you should not need these things to feel content. There is a difference between the male who puts effort into self-improvement and the male who needs to improve to shore up his shaky sense of self. The man who enjoys the journey learns from failure and looks for ways to improve. The man who needs to improve feels constant pressure to move faster and shames himself when he makes mistakes.

The 'Wanting' Addiction

There's a difference between wanting and liking. Wanting is driven by lack; liking is driven by enjoyment—and researchers have found significantly different biochemical responses between the two. "Because dopamine guides reward salience, not the hedonic impact of the reward when it actually arrives, changes in dopamine neurons and the mesolimbic dopamine system following prolonged drug use increase 'wanting' responses."[18] In other words, the moment you begin to want something, dopamine is released in the brain. You don't have to get the thing you want to achieve the rewarding feeling. All you need to do is simply start wanting.

Liking is much different. It produces endorphins and endocannabinoids, which act as neurotransmitters that provide you with a sense of pleasure, joy, and an improved sense of well-being.[19] Because "liking" does not involve

18 Patrick Anselme, "'Wanting,' 'Liking,' and Their Relation to Consciousness," *Journal of Experimental Psychology: Animal Learning and Cognition* 42, No. 2 (2016): 123–140, https://doi.org/10.1037/xan0000090.

19 Marci R. Mitchell, Kent C. Berridge, Stephen, V. Mahler, "Endocannabinoid-Enhanced 'Liking' in Nucleus Accumbens Shell Hedonic Hotspot Requires Endogenous Opioid Signals," Cannabis Cannabinoid Res 3, No. 1 (2018): 166-170, https://doi.org/10.1089/can.2018.0021.

dopamine, you will not see the addictive or compulsive behaviours that you will see when "wanting."

High achievers often spend a lot of time wanting things. They are always dreaming about who they want to become and everything they are going to have once they get there. The dopamine from "wanting" provides them the motivation and focus to make sure they stay on track. But what starts as daydreaming can quickly turn into an addiction. You begin to want for the sake of wanting. The thing that you said would finally make you happy already happened and you moved on to wanting something more.

> I believe nonstop wanting is one of the biggest reasons high achievers become addicts. Nonstop wanting mixed with a constant desire to be better is a very dangerous combination. It produces a feeling of incompleteness—an emptiness that never quite seems to be filled.

Wanting adds fuel to the fire. The dopamine crash that follows episodes of wanting puts sex addicts at a high risk of using sex to fix it. Working and wanting are the high achiever's most common sources of dopamine. So, when both are inaccessible or don't do the trick, the act itself—sex, porn, affairs—is not that far down the list.

Shapeshifting

High achievers are hard-wired to achieve greatness. As such, they tend to be hyperaware of other people and what they care about, about human culture and behavior. High achievers notice who gets picked first, who gets picked last, who has the most respect, who has the most power, who is happy, and who is stressed.

They also have a strong desire to make an impact. The challenge with being born to make an impact is that other people determine whether something is impactful. Makes sense. How much of an impact was made if nobody noticed? So, when high achievers receive praise, it indicates to them that they are on the right path. Praise encourages them to double down and do more of what everyone finds to be so impressive.

This heightened awareness of the world around them makes them experts at human interaction. By the time they enter early adulthood, these men can quickly determine how they need to show up to get what they want. Their ability to become whoever they need to be to impress other people is largely the reason they find success much faster than the people without that skill.

Successful men are rewarded for their ability to shapeshift and change their identities. They make more money, get more attention, and have access to more opportunities. As time goes on, these men get even better at impressing people and the rewards become larger.

The problem with society rewarding the ability to change who you are is that it seems like the right thing to do. While shapeshifting can be advantageous in some circumstances, most of life does not require such a performance. Furthermore, some men can maintain a firm boundary between their performance and their true self; others begin to enjoy the performance and lose sight of who they actually are. They like to be able to consistently impress others, they depend on it even, preferring that over reality. So begins a double life.

Living a double life appears harmless. You're making great money. People like you. You're winning awards and receiving compliments. How could there be anything wrong with performing if everyone seems to be benefiting from it?

Here is the problem: Living a double life opens the door to living a triple life, a quadruple life, a quintuple life, and so on.

Can someone live multiple lives and still prioritize the life they truly want? Maybe, but it's far more likely that some of these lives will begin to conflict with the life you really want. On the one hand, you may desire attention and validation from attractive women. On the other hand, you desire a marriage where all the sexual energy is preserved for you and your partner.

Your definition of success may also conflict with aspects of your dream life. The influence and impact you desire may require you to sacrifice time with your family, which threatens the close relationship you desire. This is why many successful men are susceptible to developing a sex addiction. Their lives up to this point have temporarily opened them up to compromising their values and acting like someone they're not.

This is where the concept of integrity comes into play. *The Oxford Dictionary* defines integrity as, "the state of being whole and undivided." When you are rewarded and praised for shapeshifting, the value of integrity can come into question: *If life is better when I become whoever other people want me to be, why would I want to be one thing?* The answer to this question depends on what you mean by "better." If you're looking at things from a capitalist standpoint, then yes, becoming whoever people want you to be can be advantageous. But, if you're talking about relationships, marriage, and parenting . . . constantly showing up as someone different can be disruptive, confusing, and at times frightening.

> Being able to modulate your personality to best fit those around you is an incredibly valuable skill in business. It's often what separates those who achieve massive success from those who do not. However, you do not want to lose sight of who you truly are. The truth is that you can be successful without living a double life. One would even argue that you will be even more successful when you combine this skill while maintaining your integrity.

Stay tuned for the recovery section of this book, for more . . .

The Success-Envy Paradox

According to the *Journal of Investigation in Health and Psychology*, "Envy is amplified when individuals perceive a significant gap between their achievements and those of others within their social circles. The fear of being overshadowed and experiencing a diminished sense of importance fuels resentment and animosity towards successful individuals." It's called the success-envy paradox.[20]

Even in your greatest moments people will try to convince you that you are not special; they'll call you greedy, narcissistic, and selfish. They are not necessarily being evil; they simply do not know what to do with a high achiever. People are used to being around those who choose to be victims, complain, and make excuses. So, when they are around someone who deeply believes they have been called for more in life, it's a shock to their system.

They want you to be normal and fit into one of the preestablished boxes—which is more than likely, your worst nightmare. You long to achieve; anything that tries to suppress you can be traumatizing. It goes against everything you stand for. Yet it happens to people across the globe every single day—and the system is successful 99% of the time.

This is important to put on your radar as a sex addict. Because the suppression of your uniqueness may have been the primary cause of your sex addiction. When you

20 Fabio Carraturo, Tiziana Di Perna, Viviana Giannicola, et al, "Envy, Social Comparison, and Depression on Social Networking Sites: A Systematic Review," Eur. J. Investig. Health Psychol. Educ. 13, No. 2 (2023): 364-376, https://doi.org/10.3390/ejihpe13020027.

feel as though you cannot live the life you were made to live—that your individuality, needs, motivations, and emotions have been stripped away—you feel less than human.

You become a shell of yourself, an object that exists to follow a preestablished plan. Normal looking on the outside, hollow on the inside. You were led to believe that the world would be happier if you would be like everyone else—that you need to learn how to "fit in." For most, living life this way requires something outside of themselves to numb the pain. For some, it's work, TV, video games, drugs, or alcohol. For others, it's sex and pornography.

As a high achiever, people will be envious of your success. Because of your desire to please and impress others, their envy will be a hard pill to swallow. But hear this: Their envy has nothing to do with you. Do not let the people around you turn you into someone you're not. That road will never lead you to any place you want to be.

Be nice to yourself and be honest. If you feel like you have more to offer and it has been trapped inside of you, it's worth hiring a professional to help get it out. Not only will this help resolve your sex addiction, but it may lead you to the fulfilling life you have worked so hard to create.

Fewer People to Guide

There are some things you need to learn the hard way; other things you will never learn unless someone teaches you. As the saying goes, "If you want to go fast, go alone. But, if you want to go far, go together."

This is where high achievers struggle. They are skeptical and inquisitive. Not to be confused with pessimistic and closed-minded—quite the opposite; they typically are very coachable. The problem is that they are also very selective about who they listen to. They know that their life experience is uncommon. Therefore, if they are going to seek help from someone else, that person will have to prove they understand how to help.

High achievers have their own definition of credibility. It focuses on intellect and life experience over years of schooling. Because of their own life success, they know that being good at school is very different from being good at life. This ends up being a significant challenge for sex addicts when it comes to their recovery. They may appear to be resistant to therapy, but they are not. They simply require more of an explanation before they will listen to someone else. This is why sex addicts who are high achievers thrive in a mastermind group full of like-minded men. They know how to connect the dots.

Perhaps you can relate. You have access to more money, more connections, and more confidence when it comes to finding help. But you've also found the number of people equipped to support you is much smaller. You just need to know where to look.

> To help, I've developed a tool that maps out exactly how to find the right support group that will keep you accountable, save your marriage, and achieve a full recovery. You'll find it at **successfuladdict.com/findagroup**

Boredom, Aimlessness, and Futility

From my experience, high achievers and high-net-worth men with sex addiction tend to act out in a fairly predictable way. The three things that most often cause them to seek out sex and porn are boredom, lack of direction, and a sense of futility.

High achievers hate being bored. They fill their schedule with work opportunities, self-development, and leisure activities. But there are times when being busy is not possible—it's in the silence that men find themselves bored and seeking something to occupy their busy minds.

They are used to being stimulated mentally. When they aren't working or playing, they are wanting and dreaming. At 11 p.m., it's tough to find a bigger dopamine source than sex, porn, or texting your affair partner.

The reality is that you are going to have to find a way to cure the source of your boredom. There are several good resources out there that can help. For example, Nick Trenton offers a variety of techniques to help you regulate dopamine levels and achieve greater focus, happiness, and productivity.[21] Dr. Cameron Sepah teaches how you can live life with lower levels of dopamine, which will help you dramatically in your recovery.[22] And Dr. Anna Lembke shows how you can reset the dopamine reward center of the brain (and offers hope for those bleak moments): "You'll probably feel a lot worse before you start feeling better. But stick with it—after about two weeks, the pleasure-pain see-saw in your brain will start to restore to its natural balance and you'll be able to enjoy more modest rewards, like just one scoop of ice cream or just one episode of a TV show."[23]

---

21 Nick Trenton, *Dopamine Detox: Biohacking Your Way to Better Focus, Greater Happiness, and Peak Performance* (NCTS Inc., 2021), Kindle.

22 Cameron Sepah, "The Definitive Guide to Dopamine Fasting 2.0: The Hot Silicon Valley Trend," Medium, October 28, 2019, https://medium.com/swlh/dopamine-fasting-2-0-the-hot-silicon-valley-trend-7c4dc3ba2213.

23 Anna Lembke, *Dopamine Nation: Finding Balance in the Age of Indulgence* (Dutton, 2021).

For high achievers, feeling a lack of direction is one level worse than boredom. They thrive when they know what they want and have a plan to get it. Typically, they get better at clarifying goals and executing on their action plan. Still, there are times when life throws a setback, a change of plans, or the current plan simply stops working.

At such times, you are sure to feel lost, uncertain, or behind. A lack of direction means you're off course; you don't know what to do next. Without a solid plan, you may frantically look for a solution. If you have a plan in place, you will use this nervous energy to seek help. If you don't have a plan, you might end up using sex or porn to distract you.

Feeling bored or a lack of direction are common triggers for sex addicts, but they don't hold a candle to the feeling of futility. Futility is when life feels meaningless or pointless—something that seems counterintuitive to a life full of accomplishment and above-average success. It's quite natural, actually. High achievers hold themselves to an absurdly high standard. Even a slow week can cause them to doubt their abilities.

> When the men in my recovery groups map out their timeline of acting out, it's common to see a spike during certain events: the sale of a business, months after accomplishing something difficult that took years of hard work, a loss of income, or a time of transition. Such events can result in feelings of meaninglessness or pointlessness.

Modern research has proven that the primary cause of addiction is loneliness and there's nothing lonelier than feeling like your life has no meaning. In these moments, connection with others is so important.

This notion was reinforced by the "Rat Park" studies in the 1970s. Previously, addiction research was performed on rats locked up in small cages. When given the choice between water and water laced with morphine, nearly 100% of them became addicted and died. Then, Bruce Alexander placed them in a large room called rat park, where they were free to play and socialize with other rats. The rats who were isolated in cages consumed 19 times more morphine than the rats who were in rat park.[24]

---

24 Suzanne H. Gage and Harry Sumnall, "Rat Park: How a Rat Paradise Changed the Narrative of Addiction," Addiction 144, No. 5 (2018): 917-922, https://doi.org/10.1111/add.14481.

This simple study shifted addiction treatment forever. When life feels pointless, meaningless, and lacks connection, you are more susceptible to addiction. This is why you will hear therapists, counselors, and other sex addicts tell you that the most important thing you can do for your recovery is to connect with other addicts with whom you enjoy spending time.

A good part of recovery is taking a good hard look at what you've been trying to ignore all these years. You need to be able to recognize roadblocks and setbacks—to watch out for those feelings most likely to result in acting out sexually, so you can truly recover. But, before you can truly recover, you need to get sober.

6

Your Sobriety Plan

When you hear the word "sobriety" in the addiction world, it's often spoken of as a state wherein the addiction is no more. *You want to get sober. Your wife wants you to get sober.* However, it's important to remember, it's not a switch that can be flipped. You may not want to hear it, but sobriety is a spectrum. As such, you've got to understand what it looks like, recognize where you are on it, and have a plan to help you stay or get back on track.

The Sobriety Spectrum

On one end of the sobriety spectrum is being "addict-minded;" on the other end of the spectrum is being "sober-minded."

Addict-minded ──────→ Sober-minded

At the addict-minded end of the spectrum, you are 100% driven by your addict mind. You ignore your own value system and disregard all consequences of your behavior. Since meeting your needs is your primary concern, you are not thinking about how your behaviors affect others. It's unsafe to be in a relationship with a person who is completely run by the addict mind.

On the other end of the sobriety spectrum is being sober-minded. Living sober minded means you always consider your values system first when making decisions. You choose to live in integrity over any other way of living. Before you act, you consider how your behavior may impact those around you. On the sober-minded side of the spectrum, addiction doesn't stand a chance as sober thoughts are too strong to allow harmful behaviors to occur. Being married to someone who is sober-minded makes one feel safe and secure.

While we all strive to live sober-minded, it may be physically impossible to live there 100% of the time. Everyone has moments where they let the lesser versions of themselves overpower their authentic self. That doesn't make them addict-minded, but it does move them closer to that side of the sobriety spectrum. It's not an excuse to act out; it's a sign to stay hypervigilant.

Eliminating your addict mind may never be possible. Some of the addictive neuropathways might always remain. The goal is to be so far towards the sober-minded side of the spectrum that the addict mind does not stand a chance of winning your attention. Of course, getting there doesn't happen overnight.

As much as you want (and your wife wants you) to be 100% sober right now, it doesn't work that way. In the beginning, you will be far from sober even if you are acting as such. You may be adding up sober days, but your addict mind is still stronger than your sober mind. Overcoming addiction is difficult and takes time.

When you first start your recovery work, you will be far on the addict-minded side of the sobriety spectrum. You will experience the world thinking more like an addict than someone who is sober. You might find yourself relapsing more often, because addict thoughts dominate your thinking, causing you to act out.

In the early stages, your addict mind will win your attention fairly often. This does not mean you are not making progress. It simply means your sober mind is not yet strong enough. Eventually, your sober thoughts will dominate your thinking patterns, and it will become much more difficult for your addict mind to win.

Notice I did not say impossible; just because you are sober minded more often does not mean that your addict mind is incapable of winning your attention. If you put in enough recovery work, you may be able to fight for sobriety long enough to make it through. However, most men will not make it without experiencing a relapse.[25] If this happens to you, it doesn't mean that you're an addict again. It simply means your sober mind is not yet strong enough to prevent your addict mind from winning.

Even the addicts who have developed a stronger sober mind will be faced with occasional addict thoughts that can overpower them. However, with enough recovery work, the sober mind can become strong enough to prevent addict thoughts from gaining power.

In every moment of every day, you are at some point along the recovery spectrum. You may want to be further along, but you aren't yet. All you can do is observe your addict thoughts each day and make a sobriety plan that makes you more sober-minded. Each day gets easier as

---

25 Jennifer P. Schneider, M. Debroah Corley, and Richard R. Irons, "Surviving Disclosure of Infidelity: Results of an International Survey of 164 Recovering Sex Addicts and Partners," *Sexual Addiction & Compulsivity* 5, No.3 (1998): 189-218.

you move further toward the sober side of the spectrum. But it's still a spectrum. While you are not completely an addict, you are also not completely sober.

If your wife has no interest in showing you grace during recovery, that is her right to do so. You should have been sober from the start; she has every right to demand your immediate sobriety without relapse. However, if she's open to it, you can use her help when your sober mind is not strong enough to beat your addict mind: Give her permission to hold you accountable, and come up with a system that allows you to inform her of where you are in recovery. If it's difficult to do independently, you can work with a couple's therapist to come up with a plan that works for both of you. Together, you can move safely further along the recovery spectrum until reliable sobriety is achieved. Whether you have your wife's support or not, it is your responsibility to put systems in place to avoid relapse as you work towards living on the sober-minded end of the spectrum.

Sobriety Practices

There are tons of sobriety practices, and you will have to figure out which ones will work for you. You will learn many of them throughout your recovery, but the practices themselves will not make you sober; it's the work you put into those practices that get you sober.

Sober living comes down to constructing a sobriety plan that meets your specific needs. You are going to get a lot of advice from therapists and other addicts in recovery. But they are not you. Just because it worked for them does not mean that you are going to experience the same result.

We will touch on the most common sobriety practices and why (or why they may not) work. In the end, it will be up to you to try out each strategy and modify, as needed, to meet your individual needs.

Practice 1: Adding Humanity Back In

Sex addicts dehumanize women. They turn women into objects to fulfill their sexual fantasies, masculinity, status, or human needs. To do so, the addict must first dehumanize themselves. As discussed earlier, high-achieving men have the tendency to abandon their humanity in favor of being liked, admired, and financially successful. Rather than being human (feeling their emotions, listening to their needs, and following their motivations), they turn themselves into people-pleasing machines to chase success. Disconnecting from their own humanity is what allows them to no longer see the humanity in others, thus, allowing them to use other people to get what they want.

Then, you add shame to the mix—shame is what keeps addiction going. Shame is different from guilt. Guilt is feeling bad for something you did. "I did" something bad. Shame is an identity. "I am" bad because of what I did.

Humility is defined as a modest view of one's own importance. It may not seem like it, but shame is a selfish emotion. To feel like you are worse than everyone else is no different than thinking you are better than everyone else. Whether you believe that you are better or worse, you are placing yourself above or below the humans around you. This separation from your peers is isolating and why you can be surrounded by friends and family all day yet still feel alone inside. It is much harder to be selfish when you share deep connections with other people who matter just as much as you do.

As your addiction progresses, you will progressively dehumanize yourself. As a result, you will treat yourself poorly. You may choose sex and porn over professional development. You may take unnecessary trips with the main reason being to act out sexually. At the extreme end of dehumanizing yourself, you may engage in unprotected sex or participate in illegal behavior, such as hiring prostitutes, escorts, visiting massage parlours, accidentally or intentionally engaging with a minor. These behaviors only last for a few hours, but they have the potential to ruin your life.

Connection is the best re-humanization tool. Human connection destroys shame by introducing you to the idea that you are no different from everyone else. The more connected you are to other people, the more you will realize that they also live with fears and insecurities of their own. The deeper your connections, the less shame you will feel.

To feel connected with others, you must first rehumanize yourself. Until you treat yourself like a human, you will not be able to treat anyone else like a human, which is what makes true connection possible. Humans only connect with other humans.

Practice 2: 12-Step Programs

One of the first things other addicts will suggest you do is attend 12-step meetings—not because they are effective, but because they are free and immediately accessible.

The 12-step programs will connect you with other sex addicts. Between Sexaholics Anonymous (SA) and Sex

Addicts Anonymous (SAA), there are thousands of meetings all over the world. For those who do not have a local meeting to attend, at any given moment, there is a virtual meeting you can join somewhere in the world.

Unfortunately, you get what you pay for.

These programs are member-run and rely on donations to pay their rent. Because there is no owner involved, the programs lack innovation, accountability, structure, and supervision. As an addict with your marriage on the line, the lack of urgency and organization can feel unsettling.

Because there is no facilitator onsite, the rules state that there is no crosstalk. They do this to prevent someone from providing harmful or unsolicited advice. These rules exist to create a safe place for addicts to share their experiences and feel like they are not alone in recovery. The problem with eliminating crosstalk is that it also limits the amount of connection that can be created between the men in the group. When you share that last week was the most challenging week of your life and the only response is, "Thanks Bob," it does not often result in a feeling of connectedness.

They are called "12-step programs" for a reason. Much of what is discussed at the meetings revolves around the 12 steps of recovery, originally founded by Alcoholics

Anonymous (AA). Each person shares their experience when working on each step. If the 12 steps do not resonate with you, however, these programs may not be a good fit for your recovery.

12-step programs were originally designed for substance addiction, not process addiction. There is no evidence that shows the 12-steps method is effective in treating sex addiction. This is not to say that there is no benefit from being around other addicts. However, understand that these are peer support groups and not psychotherapy.

The other big piece of the 12-step program is sponsorship. A sponsor is supposed to be someone in recovery who has more experience than the one being sponsored. The purpose of the sponsor is to walk you through the 12 steps. You are also to call your sponsor anytime you are at risk of relapse. However, because the 12-step programs are member-run, there is no training or standardization for who can be a sponsor. As a result, finding a good sponsor is very difficult. They have lives of their own and sponsoring another addict is not always something they have room for. Unfortunately, finding a sponsor who is invested in your recovery comes down to luck of the draw.

Despite the lack of research showing that these programs are effective for process addition, the 12-step programs are a go-to for sex addiction therapists and counselors. Connection is what addicts need, and these groups are full of addicts there for the same reason. However, the structure is incredibly inefficient when it comes to creating deep connections between members. The inefficiency is largely why you will not see many high achievers at 12-step meetings. Accountability and support are not built into the program. If you want support, not only will you need to ask the men in the group if they can give it to you—you will need to teach them how to do it.

I do not say this to denounce the 12-step programs. As it stands today, 12-step programs remain the easiest way to find other men with sex addiction. Simply know, it will likely be completely on you to establish connection, support, and accountability. These things will happen outside of the meetings, on your own time. I have seen men create deep relationships with other men at the meetings. I have seen men establish a support and accountability system with other members of the group. These men typically achieve sobriety faster because of the connection and support they receive. Yet it all happened outside of the 12-step program.

Like all recovery strategies, this is just one piece of the puzzle. No single recovery strategy will provide you with everything you need to overcome addiction. The 12-step programs are a great way to expand your network of addicts to connect with. But don't sit back and wait for the program to provide you with connection, support, and accountability. If you're unable to get what you need locally, try joining another group virtually. If you are still struggling to find a group of like-minded men to connect with, you may need to seek out a for-profit sex addiction recovery group that curates the support you are looking for.

Practice 3: True Connection

There is a plethora of research and psychology that supports the fact that human connection is effective in treating addiction. When it comes to sex addiction, connection is not simply effective, it's necessary.

But not any connection. It's not simply going to a 12-step meeting, smiling at others and saying "hello," and being the most well-known guy in the room. You can speak on stage and still feel alone and disconnected. I know because that was me.

True connection is difficult to put into words. It's more of a feeling you get when around others: a feeling of equality, being seen, and feeling heard. It happens when you see the humanity in another person, and you know that they see the humanity in you. By humanity, I mean the complexities, gifts, flaws, imperfections, and uniqueness that each person brings with them. Connection requires humanity on both ends of the relationship. Without it, no connection is possible.

Intimacy disorders affect all areas of life. The inability to truly connect with others usually originates in childhood when it became advantageous to look better and put on a show for other people.

For most high achievers, putting on a show for others is what you do best. When performed for decades, this practice can lead you to forget who you really are. The majority of the world falls into this category—it's not just sex addicts—which is why true connection has become so rare. According to the Pew Research Center, only 53% of people in the U.S. report having one good friend.[26] This is the lowest it has been since they began collecting data.

---

26 Isabel Goddard, "What Does Friendship Look Like in America?" Pew Research Center (2023): https://www.pewresearch.org/short-reads/2023/10/12/what-does-friendship-look-like-in-america/.

In an era dominated by social media, we're more connected than ever. The irony is that we live in the most disconnected time in history. We now spend far more time thinking about getting better and competing with others than the generations before. In a world that feels like a contest, we can easily fail to see the humanity in ourselves let alone the people around us. Connection has no place in a world where you are striving to be better than everyone else.

All that to say, true connection is not as easy as it might seem.

Yet as a sex addict, you need true connection if you want to achieve long-term sobriety. To get to that place, you will need to learn how to press pause on your efforts to constantly manage your image. That may help you in business, but not when trying to connect with your wife.

The truth is that everyone is equal. No human will ever be better than another human. It doesn't matter how much money they have or what they have accomplished. A human's value does not fluctuate based on their bank account balance or the number of awards received. Competition is a man-made construct that divides us. As long as you are trying to be better than everyone else, you will always feel disconnected and isolated. It's lonely at the top. Only one person can be up there. As an addict, is that really where you want to be?

Practice 4: Disclosing Your Secrets

Addiction thrives in secrecy. Disclosing your secrets is key to getting sober. The best way to begin practicing this is in therapy with a counselor. Therapists, especially Certified Sex Addiction Therapists (CSAT), are trained to work with sex and pornography addicts. Nothing you can say will surprise them. It's quite the opposite. The more you disclose to them the better they will be able to help you in recovery.

While therapy is a great place to start, sharing your unwanted sexual behaviors with other men is even more effective when it comes to reducing shame. This can be done at a sex addiction intensive or retreat. Something changes in an addict when they share their deepest secrets with others. But the real change happens when you see that the other men in the group love you more after you share your secrets with them.

Then there's your wife. Your wife will never be happy to hear about a slip or a relapse. Yet continued lying is a sure way to prevent regaining her trust. Getting everything out on the table is important if you want to achieve long-term sobriety and mend your relationship. Sex addiction therapists call it a "therapeutic full disclosure:" when you reveal everything your wife wants to know about your sexual acting out. Some wives don't want to know much; others want to know everything. It's their right to know everything that has happened during your relationship. You should want that as well. Disclosure is not just for your wife's sanity.

If you want to overcome this addiction, you will need to get into the habit of disclosing information and taking ownership of your actions. Telling the truth is hard when you're an addict. It's not your truth, it's the truth of the addiction. The real you wants this addiction out of your life (that's why you are reading this book). The addict mind wants to act out sexually. It is not fun to admit to something that you did sexually when you didn't want to do it in the first place. However, you still did it, and you need to own that. You will find that disclosure gets easier the more you do it.

So, remember: The things that are disclosed will lose their power over you. The things that you continue to hide are more likely to cause you to relapse.

Practice 5: Mindfulness

The first thing most addicts do to promote sobriety is install porn blockers and delete anything from their phone that may lead to acting out sexually . . .

You cannot go to war with your addiction and expect to win.

As long as the beliefs exist that make you act compulsively, you will always find a way to act out. Yes, barriers can buy you some time to avoid a relapse, but they are far from foolproof.

Every sex addict knows better. Yet they still do things they do not want to do. One of the most frustrating and shameful things about addiction is that it seems to happen without your control. The dreaded question: "What were you thinking?" Truth is, you were not thinking. Your mind was on a mission to feed the addiction.

You cannot control your mind. However, you can become more mindful. Mindfulness is not mind control but rather a practice of being conscious or aware of your thoughts. Thoughts are just thoughts. Alone, they have no value or significance. However, when thoughts are acted on, they become actions. Actions have consequences. When it comes to sex addiction, these consequences can be divorce, disease, pregnancy, a destroyed career, family, and reputation.

This is where mindfulness comes into play. Mindfulness practices allow you to observe your thoughts. You're probably familiar with some of the most common: meditation, journaling, and breathing exercises. These practices work by slowing down your mind just enough for you to notice your thoughts. Even doing this for a few minutes can make a huge difference as it gives you the opportunity to determine where thoughts like these may lead you.

Mindfulness does not have to be anything in particular. The goal is to choose a practice or activity that slows your mind down enough for you to notice what you are thinking and feeling. These practices do not cure sex addiction. However, they do help slow things down enough to buy you some time to decide if you really do want to do what you think you want to do. Addicts always report that their mind was hijacked, and they lost control. Mindfulness practices can help prevent your mind from being hijacked by the addict and allow more room for sober thoughts.

Practice 6: Routine

We've already touched on the big three: boredom, lack of direction, and futility; a life that feels mundane, repetitive, or meaningless goes against the DNA of a high achiever . . . and is a common cause of acting out sexually.

Routine is your biggest ally.

As a high achiever, you are hardwired to achieve. Give you a schedule that is guaranteed to bring success and chances are good you will execute it. The challenge: It's hard to stick to routine. Life is ever evolving. Vacations, work travel, busy seasons, slow seasons—your routine will need to change and adapt.

Routine is something that you should be discussing with your recovery group and your therapist. If your wife is comfortable helping with this, you can ask her to keep an eye on your routine and let you know when changes may need to be made.

Practice 7: Emotional Regulation

We all experience negative emotions at one time or another: anxiety, stress, fear, worry, anger, panic, regret, hopelessness, feeling less than, feeling behind, feeling as if you are wasting your time—basically any emotion we want to go away. In the world of psychology, the experience of negative emotions is called dysregulation or feeling dysregulated.

Most high achievers do not believe they experience many negative emotions. Their life is pretty good. Understandably, their life is pretty good in comparison to most people in the world. They typically aren't depressed. They usually have a way to effectively manage stress. However, to say they don't feel many negative emotions is simply not true.

A common thread amongst most of my successful clients is a feeling of not being good enough yet. They feel behind; they aren't moving fast enough; they don't have enough money. They feel they've been passed up; they deserve a seat at the table; they should be further ahead than they are today. These feelings of inadequacy have the potential to cause significant dysregulation.

The thing is we're hardwired at birth to fulfill our full potential. To do so, we need to make decisions in a peaceful and stable environment. We are biologically driven to resolve negative feelings, to get back to a neutral place, for the best chance of fulfilling our needs. In the addiction recovery world, it's called emotional regulation. We must learn how to regulate our emotions effectively if we want to achieve long-term sobriety.

There are many ways to regulate your emotions. Some are effective and sustainable, such as connecting with friends, helping others, asking for help, participating in a peer group. Others—such as fishing for compliments, competition, starting a new business, looking at porn— are only temporarily effective and will require you to repeat them to achieve emotional regulation. Developing healthy emotional regulation strategies is key to your recovery and saving your marriage.

We'll cover various regulation strategies, as well as the healthy order in which to use them, in coming chapters. For now, a few basics . . .

Dr. Stephen Porges's work revolutionized addiction treatment and emotional regulation with his polyvagal theory.[27] In the polyvagal model, the body uses three systems to regulate its emotions: the social engagement system (your first line of defense), the sympathetic nervous system (your second line of defense), and the dorsal vagal system (your third line of defense).

Your First Line of Defense in Emotional Regulation

The social engagement system regulates your emotions through connection with other people. When you experience a negative emotion and use your social engagement system, you will express how you are feeling to someone else, and they will do their best to help you.

---

27 "What is the Polyvagal Theory?", Polyvagal Institute, accessed September 15, 2024, https://www.polyvagalinstitute.org/whatispoly vagaltheory.

Social regulation is your first line of defense against negative emotions, and science shows it's hardwired from birth. As a child, you instinctually go to others for help when you are feeling dysregulated. Whether you continue to go that route, largely depends on your experience.

If your parents showed early on that your emotions matter and that people want to help take away negative feelings, chances are good, you will continue to seek others out. Children who are taught that it is okay to express their emotions in a healthy manner will often grow up to be adults who can communicate their emotions effectively. Because of that, you build a long list of friends, colleagues, and mentors whom you can rely on to regulate negative emotions. Depending on what's causing distress, you then seek help from the person you believe can best provide the comfort, advice, or help needed.

Unfortunately, you may not have been taught to express emotions as a child. Maybe your parents looked at your emotions as immature or irrelevant—maybe they considered your emotions a burden or nuisance. Maybe they were trying to be helpful; they had an agenda for what they believed would result in you living a better life or becoming a better person. Whatever the reason, you stopped expressing your emotions because you learned they don't matter as much as following your parent's plan.

Unfortunately, just because you grow up and attend college, make a lot of money, and practice good financial habits, doesn't mean you live a peaceful life feeling emotionally regulated. Failing to develop social regulation strategies often leads to frequent irritability, poor conflict resolution skills, and difficulty in relationships.

It's safe to assume, as a sex addict, you do not use a social regulation strategy as often as you should. You're not alone. It's a growing problem in the United States. According to the World Economic Forum, people in the U.S. have far fewer close friends than 30 years ago. Just 13% of U.S. adults say they have 10 or more close friends, compared with 33% of those surveyed in 1990.[28] Yet allowing people to help you navigate hard times is the healthiest and easiest way to regulate your emotions back to neutral. Social regulation strategies have no negative side effects. As a matter of fact, once you learn to reach out to others as soon as you feel dysregulated, you'll likely experience negative emotions for much shorter periods and be able to solve your problems faster than those who are unable to use a social regulation strategy.

---

28 "Friendships: Less Is Now More," World Economic Forum, November 3, 2022, https://www.weforum.org/agenda/2022/11/friendships-less-is-now-more/.

Your Second Line of Defense

So, what happens if you are unable to regulate socially? What if you are alone and have nobody to talk to? What if the person you talk to doesn't know how to help in a way that regulates you? What if you don't like expressing your emotions and asking for help?

If social regulation fails to neutralize your negative emotions, you will need to rely on your second line of defense, your sympathetic nervous system. Your sympathetic nervous system gets you ready for action. Rather than socially regulating through connection (your first line of defense), the sympathetic response is a cry for help. It's your body's response to feeling unsafe, unseen, unheard, or uncared for.

Here you will experience emotions of fear, anxiety, irritation, anger, panic, and frustration. While our society has labelled these emotions as bad, inappropriate, or childish, they are very normal and quite necessary. When you experience these feelings, your body is telling you that the people around you are not currently able to help. These feelings prompt you to further explain yourself to the people around you or find someone who is better qualified to assist you.

Your sympathetic response to distress is unsustainable and your body will not tolerate it for long. You can only feel stressed, frustrated, or angry for so long before you are going to need to do something to make the feelings go away. If your negative emotions are not regulated, they may continue to escalate and worsen in severity. At the peak of your sympathetic response, you will experience rage.

Rage is defined as uncontrollable anger that can be expressed in many ways, and it doesn't have to be expressed outwardly. Some people will throw things, punch walls. Others will internalize the rage and take it out on themselves through negative self-talk or even self-harm. While rage is often considered the most shameful expression of anger, it's really your body's final cry for help. It's easy to look at the person raging in anger and become scared of them or shame them for how they are acting. In reality, the best thing to do for this person would be to let them know that you see them and hear them.

If you're married, you probably experienced your wife's rage after she discovered your sex addiction. You may have concluded that she hates you or that she is on the verge of asking for a divorce. Tammy Gustafson, counselor and founder of the Betrayal Healing Conference, suggests the opposite, "When a wife shows her anger, she is still engaged in the relationship to allow her blood to boil. I fear for relationships where the wife no longer gets angry. Silent wives have shut their hearts out of their relationship."[29]

Rage, and your wife's willingness to express it, means she still cares very much about you. If she didn't care, she would not be experiencing a sympathetic nervous system reaction. So, the next time it happens, try to recognize her emotions for what they are—a cry for your attention, love, and support.

Your Third Line of Defense

If you are unable to find anyone who can help you feel better about your situation, you will seek out methods that do not involve human connection. When it seems that you are on your own, you will rely on your third line of defense against negative emotions, your dorsal vagal system.

The dorsal vagal system takes a completely different approach. Unlike your social engagement system and your

---

29 "The Importance of Anger after Betrayal," Live Free Counseling, accessed November 16, 2024, https://livefreecounseling.com/the-importance-of-anger-after-betrayal.

sympathetic nervous system, your dorsal nervous system does not waste time feeling or expressing emotion. To the dorsal nervous system, nobody cares how you feel. So, why would you bother wasting your time feeling fear, anxiety, irritation, anger, panic, and frustration? These feelings only exhaust you and slow you down. You're better off putting your energy into something that has been proven to work.

Using self-regulation strategies over social-regulation strategies to resolve negative emotions opens the door to addiction. When you self-regulate, you limit yourself to the regulation strategies you believe are the most effective. Unfortunately, we are unreliable when it comes to choosing the most effective emotional regulation strategy. Our chosen strategies may have costly side effects that we are not considering—or we choose to do it anyway.

When you use your dorsal nervous system to regulate, you don't experience emotions for longer than a few seconds. Instead, you feel numb, dissociated, and shut down. You might call this mental state "going dorsal." Many successful men have chosen to go dorsal to feel less so they can do more. It's the "lone wolf," "me against the world," and "fuck you" mentality.

When compared to the exhausting emotions felt in your sympathetic response, going dorsal feels so much easier. When dorsal, none of that stuff pissing you off matters anymore. You don't let anything bother you or anyone else get in your way. You get to work, play, go wherever you want, and do whatever you want. But there's a catch to this seemingly blissful existence. When nothing matters enough to bother you, nothing matters enough to inspire you either.

That's the problem with going dorsal. It is not selective. Either everything matters or nothing matters. To not let your wife's emotions bother you, you must make your wife's emotions not matter; to ignore how much time you are wasting watching porn, you must devalue your time; to treat sex workers as objects, you must make their lives matter less than yours.

Going dorsal feels better than living with the pain of anxiety, fear, frustration, anger, and panic. This is the scary thing about going dorsal, it feels "right." The regulation you feel is very similar to using your first line of defense, your social engagement system. But not caring doesn't make the pain go away. The underlying issue is still there, and it will be there until you resolve it. The reason you go dorsal is because you have not found a way to resolve the source of your negative emotions.

But the only way to resolve a problem you are unable to resolve is by getting help from someone who knows how to help you solve it. Going dorsal prevents you from using your social regulation strategies—and that will cause you to live with the pain even longer . . . which will increase the likelihood of you going dorsal. This is the vicious cycle that typically leads to addiction. Because of the potential for negative side effects, your body knows only to use your dorsal vagal system for regulation as a last resort. Unfortunately, sex addicts have learned to override their bodies natural process. As a result, they use their dorsal nervous system as their primary way of regulating negative emotions.

See It Like It Is

You probably noticed that being able to rely upon your first line of defense is largely due to how your parents dealt with your emotions. But let's make it clear right now: Your inability to socially regulate is not your parent's fault. It's more of a cultural norm. It's normal for parents to force their beliefs on their kids, to want their children to make them proud and live up to their expectations, to praise behavior that meets their desires, and to punish that which doesn't.

Chances are good that you see nothing wrong with this type of parenting, as well. Which is exactly the point. It has become normal to make your kids better. But what parents don't realize is that we are micromanaging a human being who has needs, desires, and dreams of their own. Rather than raising them to become who they were born to be, we train them to become wealthy, successful, and productive members of society.

John Driggs, social worker and author of the book *Intimacy Between Men* writes, "After 18 months, a child begins to have a separate sense of self from parents and he needs a more mature form of love from his parents, one that respects and helps develop his individuality. Parents who overparent their older children may indirectly undermine their children's emerging maturity and separateness."[30] The overparenting message is clear. *We don't care who you are. Be who we want you to be.* This message teaches children at a very young age to abandon social-regulation strategies and rely on self-regulation to make their way through life.

Parents often say statements like:

- "I know you hate soccer practice. But you need to go. Get in the car."

---

30 John H. Driggs, *Intimacy Between Men: How to Find and Keep Gay Love Relationships* (Penguin, 1991).

- "I don't care if the other boys at school get to do it. I'm telling you no."

- "Suck it up. Life is hard and you don't always get to have it your way."

While common, they really shouldn't be. Without explanation, they leave the child to wonder why they would express their emotions if nobody seems to care. I bring it up because my clients often say, "I had wonderful parents and no childhood trauma to speak of." The common parenting statements above may not be "bad parenting," but they certainly do not promote the child's future use of social-regulation strategies.

Ways parents harm their child's ability to socially regulate include:

- Saying one thing to the child, but doing another, thinking the child won't notice.

- Forcing their beliefs on the child and punishing the child if they don't adopt their beliefs.

- Telling the child that they should work hard to be better.

- Rewarding the child for what he does, rather than who he is as a person.

- Excluding the child from the rest of the family if the child's behavior doesn't match the parent's desires.

- Enforcing strict household rules that primarily serve their beliefs rather than keeping the child safe.

- Shaming, gaslighting, and making the child question personal beliefs that go against the family's beliefs.

- Telling the child that certain emotions are weak or childish.

- Refusing to express their own emotions or being emotionally unavailable to the child.

Such examples are consistent with parents who lack attunement. Psychologists define attunement as the ability to pick up on the feelings and emotions of others, which means those who lack it, tend to focus on their own feelings, assuming everyone else feels similarly to them. Parents who lack attunement will overlook their child's emotions and consequently teach the child that their emotions are less important.

According to Dr. Michael Barta, author of the book *Trauma Induced Sex Addiction*, growing up with parents who lack emotional attunement is the number one cause of sex addiction.[31] This is believed to be because children lack a role model for healthy emotional expression and regulation. Growing up in a house where emotions are not valued, or even recognized, will result in a poorly developed social regulation system, which makes one more susceptible to developing an addiction.

Chances are good that you experienced many of the parenting failures listed above. You don't need to experience all of them to have developed poor social-regulation strategies. Depending on your personality, even one of them can cause your social engagement system significant harm. This does not mean your parents were bad. It means they were normal. However, as it stands today, normal parenting does not prepare a child to function in the world in a healthy sustainable way. Without a functional social engagement system, you will constantly need something outside yourself to keep you emotionally regulated. For some, that need will turn into a sex addiction.

---

31 Michael Barta, *TINSA: A Neurological Approach to the Treatment of Sex Addiction* (CreateSpace Independent Publishing Platform, 2017).

Sobriety is all about relapse prevention. There are always weaknesses in the armour. Life will always bring its ups and downs and you cannot rely on armour alone to keep you sober. Recovery is the goal. With recovery, you don't need as much armour to keep you safe. You will want to keep it with you for additional protection. But you stand a much greater chance of achieving long-term sobriety when you have recovery to stand on.

7

Your Recovery Plan

Sobriety is about doing things to prevent you from acting out. Recovery is the opposite. It is about undoing the things that make you act out. Sobriety is temporary. Recovery can be permanent—if you do the work.

Recovery will end up being the best thing that's ever happened to you. Yes, addiction is ugly. But all addictions are masking things that need attention. The men who come to my retreats leave feeling so thankful that their addiction has forced them to dive deep into themselves. I have seen men create marriages that were far better than anything they had before their wife discovered their compulsive behavior. I have seen men open new businesses that bring a deep sense of fulfillment . . . men who have found purpose . . . men headed in the direction they have been longing for their entire life.

Recovery is a journey that does not have to be about sadness and regret. You can learn from the past and create something even better. Recovery is about being who you were supposed to be in the first place. It is a fresh start and a new beginning. If you use this time to look past the addiction, deep inside of yourself you will see things that have been ignored.

Many addicts remember at least one moment when they ignored "the call." The call is a feeling you get when something needs to be done. It happens when you are off course or ignoring what you were designed to do. Recovery is your opportunity to answer that call.

Recovery is about re-examining your life, changing your mind, and updating your beliefs.

High achievers often believe they like their worldview and sense of self. They like the idea that more money will make them happy because they know how to make more money. They like the idea that buying nice things, taking luxurious vacations, winning awards, and being lusted after makes them successful because it's a convenient story. However, these stories are not based on truth. Nobody said success in these areas would make you happy. This world is set up for capitalism, not happiness. If you want to recover, you need to learn how to play the game and not allow it to play you.

What You Need

Recovery is a return to self. Every human being was designed with a purpose. In a perfect world, everyone would grow up discovering their purpose and learning how to use it to benefit the lives of others. In doing so, they would feel a sense of fulfillment and peace.

But this is not how life goes. Oftentimes, kids are not raised to find their purpose in life. They are told to become financially successful—then do their best to be happy. Parents and teachers mean well. They are trying to be supportive and encouraging by telling kids how to make money and achieve great things. Instead, they're teaching to abandon true self in favor of succeeding (as society has defined success).

I have read a lot of books on psychology and spent a lot of time studying the world's religions. Never once have they stated money or material success will result in fulfillment. "Money can't buy happiness," yet we are determined to try.

Perhaps the first step in understanding what you truly need is to understand the definition of fulfillment. It's "the achievement of something desired, promised, or predicted; the meeting of a requirement or condition." Read that again: It's predicted; it's a requirement. Humans have been designed perfectly to fulfill their needs and find their purpose.

Psychologists have been researching fulfillment and purpose for hundreds of years, including my favorite, Abraham Maslow. According to Maslow, humans are hard-wired (or pre-programmed) with the following hierarchy of needs:

At the base of the pyramid, we have our physiological needs. These are all about basic survival. Just above the base, we have our safety needs. These give us a sense of stability such as financial security, having access to the support of others, and feeling stabilized mentally. Above safety is the need for love and belonging. Humans have the need to feel connected and to belong to a tribe. The level above that is our need for esteem. Humans need to feel recognized and appreciated by others. We need to feel like a valuable member of society and that people would miss us if we were gone. We want to be seen, heard, and know that our opinion matters. At the top of Maslow's hierarchy is self-actualization. This is the need to discover and express self. We all have a deep desire to know who we are and what our purpose is. We have the need to express ourselves and what we believe.

Maslow's findings explain human behavior perfectly. Humans are hardwired to survive at all costs. Once you know that you will survive, your attention shifts towards creating a life full of stability, connection, and recognition. Once you know that you can bring value to relationships and society, your attention will shift towards self-actualization.

Maslow also discovered that humans become increasingly less motivated to fulfill the lower needs on the pyramid as they become met. However, he found the opposite with self-actualization. The more you discover your unique abilities, the more motivated you are to develop them further; the more people you impact using your unique abilities, the more people you want to help. Unlike the lower four needs on the pyramid, your motivation to further self-actualize increases the more you do it.

Why are you designed to move on to other areas of focus once safety, love, and esteem are met, when they seem so important? Why do you never get enough self-actualization—why will you never stop seeking and expressing your true self?

Because becoming yourself is the greatest gift you have to offer.

That's why it feels so good to express your beliefs, feelings, and opinions with others; that's why it feels so bad when you pretend to be someone you're not, and when you spread ideas that have nothing to do with who you really are. You have been designed to seek out and express yourself . . . your true self.

Your early life was spent achieving safety and seeking belonging. You shifted your focus to recognition for your skills and accomplishments. On the outside, you may appear to have it all; but on the inside, you're restless, bored, and discontent.

This is normal. As you achieve the needs on the bottom four levels of Maslow's hierarchy, you are meant to become bored and less motivated. There's nothing wrong with you. You aren't jaded or spoiled or damaged. It's your programming telling you to spend more time discovering who you are and looking for ways to share your purpose with others.

You have a unique design that will guide you to your purpose, if only you let it. By understanding how your design has played out in your life, you'll understand what your life has been preparing you for. If you're not where you want to be, if the life you pursued and created isn't making you happy, the issue isn't that you need to learn more, read more, or prepare more. The issue isn't that you must achieve more, win more, wow more. The issue is that you need to understand your design. It will continue to pull you towards your purpose until you live in a way that honors it.

Sex addiction can easily crop up when you are not honoring your design. It's often a coping mechanism used to shift your attention away from the thoughts and feelings that result from living out of alignment.

Your body knows when you are not living in a way that will allow you to fulfill your full potential. No feeling is more unpleasant than knowing you are falling short.

> Sex, pornography, and affairs are the distractions. Ultimately, you need to get back on course. It's your life's purpose to be who you were designed to be. Anything short will result in pain and dissatisfaction.

Your Identity

If you could flip a switch to accelerate your recovery, it would be changing your identity. The concept of an identity is how a person determines who they are as an individual and how they are seen by others. Everyone has a concept of who they are. It's not possible to be alive without a sense of personal identity.

Your identity is life's gatekeeper. It is who you think you are. It dictates what you can do, what you can't do, and what you are capable of. You will never outpace your identity. This is why I say that changing your identity is the fastest way to accelerate your recovery.

Sexually compulsive behavior happens to a person who allows it to happen. While it may not feel like you are allowing yourself to act out sexually, if it's happening, you are allowing it to happen. In the sex addiction field, you'll hear it described as justification, rationalization, and minimization. It's identifying as a person who *needs* to engage in these sexual behaviors.

Your identity will fluctuate. There will be times when you identify as someone you're proud of. You'll feel resourceful, grateful, valued, and capable. These are typically the times when it's easy for you to act sober.

On the flip side, there will be days when you identify as someone you are unsatisfied with. Someone who is too old, too fat, not successful or doing enough. You'll feel behind, unsatisfied, unattractive, or filled with regret. These are typically times when being sober becomes difficult and relapse is much more likely.

It's the fluctuation in your identity that gets you into trouble. When you are identifying as someone you are proud of, you don't let things bother you. When you are identifying as someone less than you want to be, you will take everything personally and get defensive.

You can see how your identity may cause you problems. For starters, if you have a misconstrued sense of self, it's likely you live a life that is miles away from how you were designed to live. Secondly, your view of how other people see you may be inaccurate. If so, it will force your misconstrued sense of self to do a bunch of things that have nothing to do with being happy and successful. Even a small deviation in your sense of self or view of the world can lead to massive misalignment over the course of your life.

It may not seem like a choice, but you do choose your identity. Your parents and peers may comment about who they think you are, but in the end, you decide if they were right or wrong. You and you alone decide who you are in this world.

> With high achievers there are common identities that can cause them to engage in compulsive sexual behavior:
>
> - I am more valuable when women find me attractive.
>
> - I am more confident when attractive women want to sleep with me.
>
> - I am happier when I am having exciting and frequent sex.
>
> - I am more accomplished when more women choose me over other men.

"I am" statements are very powerful. They make up your sense of identity. Typically, they are never spoken aloud. They live in your subconscious mind but have a significant influence on your concept of personal identity and how you believe others see you.

Changing the flawed parts of your identity will be the best thing you can do for your recovery. The problem is that your identity is the hardest thing to change. This is because it doesn't feel like a choice. It feels like who you truly are.

If you have always believed yourself to be the way you are, it makes sense that you would be unaware that you might be someone different. This is the challenge with the concept of identity. Nobody prepares you to make such a big decision. In fact, nobody even tells you that it's a choice. You formed your first concept of personal identity when you were a child. Most likely, it was never updated. That means you've lived a life bound to an identity that was poorly informed and likely miles away from who you are meant to be.

> The goal is to tie your identity to the person you were designed to be.

Is your current identity who you truly are? That is what you need to figure out. It always starts with awareness. It's impossible to change something without knowing what needs to change. The best way to see the flaws is to first examine your belief system. Since your identity is the gatekeeper, your beliefs may not be your own.

Beliefs

Whether consciously or unconsciously, you are continually choosing which thoughts to believe. Of the millions of beliefs out there, it's up to you to choose the truest. While you might think the choice is yours, that's not always the case. If your chosen identity is not who you truly are, then your true self is not making the decisions.

It's a crazy concept to wrap your head around. Your identity picks the beliefs it finds valid. And in those moments, you will act in alignment with those beliefs. If they see value in certain sexual behaviors, then you may find yourself engaging in them.

Your true self may be at odds with the identity you're currently living. In which case, each will have its own set of beliefs. For example, one identity wants to be a faithful husband and a man of integrity, while the other feels justified in finding ways to meet unmet sexual needs (even if that means temporarily violating their integrity).

Examining your beliefs is the easiest way to expose the identity behind the act. When you make a mistake or do something that you are not proud of, take a moment and write down the beliefs that must be true for that behavior to occur.

For example, if you relapse and look at pornography, your beliefs may be:

- It's not that bad, all guys are doing it.
- It's just porn. It's not the same as cheating.
- My wife doesn't need to know everything. My sexuality is my business.
- It was just one time. She doesn't need to know.

Now, consider what kind of person has such beliefs. It's someone who cares more about short term pleasure than the long-term effects of pornography on our society. Someone who believes that objectifying women is normal and there's nothing wrong with it. Someone who believes that it's okay to lie if you disagree with the other person's opinion.

See how those beliefs tell a story about the person believing them? If you become a master of examining your beliefs, you will eventually become a master of changing your identity. And, if you become a master at changing your identity, you can choose one that doesn't act out sexually—one that never bends the truth or compromises his integrity, or one that thinks deeply before he acts to make sure he doesn't hurt himself or anyone he loves.

Selling Your Identities

Changing your identity is an art. Outstanding counselors and therapists are good at changing problematic identities. Oftentimes, they'll be so good you won't even notice. If you want to achieve long-term sobriety, you will need to master the art of changing your problematic identities.

Notice it's "changing" your identities rather than "destroying" them. Going to war with them will not work. Anytime you go to war with something, it never goes well. The best example of this is parenting teenagers. Tell a teenager not to do something and it will make them want to do it even more. Your identities are no different. They like the way they think. Some of them are extremely defensive and resistant to change.

Your identity wants what it wants, and it will always find a way to get it. The only way you will be able to stop it is if you can sell it on a superior alternative. But before you try to sell it, you first need to understand what it is your identity wants.

For example, let's say that your current identity wants attention and validation from attractive women. Tell him to stop, and he will probably be uninterested. Instead, you need to first understand why he wants their attention. Ask questions:

- What does it mean if attractive women do not give you their attention?

- If you never got attention from attractive women again, would you be okay?

- What is the significance of their attention? What does it mean when attractive women give men their attention?

Asking questions will give insight into what he's trying to achieve. Dig deep enough, and you'll eventually find the key: He feels insignificant without their attention. Significance is what he is after.

So, if you are going to ask him to stop what makes him feel significant, you'll need to sell him on a superior strategy. Superior does not always mean "better." Sometimes superior simply means sustainable, longer lasting, or without negative consequences.

For this example, you might propose a few alternatives:

- Is it possible that significance is achieved by accomplishing hard things that few men are willing to do?

- What if using women to make you feel significant actually exposes your insecurity, therefore, making you less significant?

- What if significance is not measured by how many women find you attractive, but how many people will miss you when you're gone?

With enough alternative beliefs, you may be able to get him to question his belief system. Remember, the goal is to get your identities on the same team—on your team—and stop using sex as their go-to strategy.

Selling your identity on a superior strategy is very difficult to do on your own. This is because you likely view the world through many of the same beliefs, which makes it difficult to make meaningful change.

At my sex addiction retreats, the power of a group helps my clients see what they are unable to see on their own. No two attendees have the exact same beliefs or identities. This allows the other men in the group to see the blind spots.

Oftentimes, one of the group members will say something that finally bridges the gap in a thought process. Hearing these alternative beliefs spoken by other high achievers is what makes the mastermind effect so powerful. In one weekend, you can accomplish what would have otherwise taken you years in recovery.

Being aware of the beliefs that you are unaware of will change how you experience life. Acknowledging alternative beliefs will decrease the power your identities have over your life. Once you stop believing your old beliefs, you will finally be able to change your identity to something that better serves you. This is how you remove compulsive sexual behavior from your life . . . changing one belief at a time until recovery is achieved.

Your Emotions

Because many of your beliefs were created by an identity that doesn't resemble the real you, they are often unreliable. This means that you may have to look elsewhere for the truth. Well, you're in luck. There is one aspect of truth you can access, regardless of how difficult it is to separate your current state of existence from the life you were designed to lead: your emotions.

Your emotions are the only thing in your current reality that you can count on to give you reliable feedback.

I believe emotions serve one purpose, and that's to guide you towards a reality that will allow you to fulfill your full potential.

You can always count on your emotions to guide you back to a reality that will fulfill you. Eckhart Tolle, author of *The Power of Now*, refers to emotions as "signposts that lead to awakening."[32]

Emotions arise in response to the reality that you believe you are living in. You will experience an emotion anytime there is further action needed. If the emotion is negative, it means you need to "do less" of what brought on the unpleasant emotion. If the emotion is positive, it means you need to "do more" of what brought on the enjoyable emotion.

For example, let's say you compared yourself to those you admire, early in your career. Rather than appreciating them for what they have accomplished, you put yourself down for not being like them. *I'm not as talented as them. I will never accomplish what they have. Nobody will ever respect me like they do them.* This comparison will always result in feelings of despair, hopelessness, and disappointment.

However, as awful as those feeling are, they are telling you that this reality will not allow you to become who you need to be. The purpose of those emotions is not to remind you of your worthlessness. The purpose is to guide you towards another path.

Once you focus on your purpose, you'll start hearing the messages from your emotions differently: *In a*

---

32 Eckhart Tolle, *The Power of Now: A Guide to Spiritual Enlightenment* (New World Library, 2004).

reality where you are not talented, accomplished, and respectable . . . you will never become the person you have been designed to be. It's true. You are unable to accomplish much when you're playing small and scared of looking stupid. When you choose to live in a reality where you're skilled, knowledgeable, and gifted, you'll feel more confidence, power, and determination.

The story you tell yourself about your reality will determine the emotions you feel. Here's another example: You get cut off in the parking lot by someone who takes "your" spot—the one for which you have been waiting for five minutes, with your turn signal on . . . and this man, who has not been waiting, sneaks right in. *It's unfair; this man obviously has no respect or sense of civic responsibility!* You feel the emotion of anger.

Now, the emotion of anger does not exist to make you angrier or to take your feelings out on others. It's a result of the story you told yourself about the other driver. You got angry because you believe that you live in a world that is unfair, and people have no respect for one another. The belief is that you will suffer in a world where people don't care about others. The reality may be that the other driver just wanted to park his car as bad as you did. Maybe he didn't even see you. He has no ill will towards you and likely is just as good of a person as you are. In this reality, you will not experience anger. Instead, you will simply search for another parking spot and enjoy the music on the radio.

Another common emotion is the feeling of regret and guilt. You made a decision in the past that caused you and another person a lot of pain. Thinking back to this past event haunts you to this day and in many ways still causes you pain. You tell yourself how foolish that decision was—that only someone stupid would do something like that. If everyone knew about that mistake, nobody would ever trust you or take you seriously. Or so you think. The emotion you feel is a deep sense of guilt and regret. You attach a story to this emotion. If you feel this way, it must mean that you should be ashamed of yourself; you should make sure nobody ever finds out about what you did.

The problem with this story is that you are misinterpreting the purpose of this awful feeling. The pit you feel in your stomach is in response to you telling yourself that you are stupid and that you should hide. But this is simply the story you decided to tell yourself. The truth behind this guilt emotion is that you will never reach your full potential in a world where you are less than others. You will never feel fulfilled if you are holding back and hiding from opportunities that require your unique abilities.

The mind has a way of corrupting the message within your emotions. When you hear these voices in your head telling you how to feel, just remember that this is only one point of view. The key is to allow your emotions to guide you by questioning the current beliefs and consider what other alternatives exist. One of these new beliefs will contain the answer that your emotions are helping you look for.

How to Use Your Emotions

Unlearning what you have been told about emotions can be challenging. So, allow me to help you. All emotions are equal. Happiness is no better or worse than the feeling of anxiety. Both are telling you where to go to achieve fulfillment. One emotion is telling you to turn right, the other is telling you to go another half mile then turn left. Things begin to go wrong when you try to pursue happiness and avoid sadness.

Happiness is one of millions of emotions. Emotions are designed to tell you something; they fade away once you take action. So, chasing them is pointless. This is why chasing happiness never results in becoming happy. It's impossible to be happy all the time as this emotion is reserved to reward you for creating a reality that honors who you were designed to be.

If you have an attachment to being happy then you will become sad when this feeling leaves you. You will judge yourself for no longer feeling happy and may even conclude that something is wrong with you. Instead, next time you feel the emotion of happiness, enjoy that moment. Maybe later you can become curious about why that feeling came over you and what it can teach you about yourself.

Many admit to feeling numb and unable to feel their emotions. It's not because they lack emotions. It's because their mind is so quick at distracting them, they don't get the chance to see the emotion at all. Feelings are quickly turned into labels and judgments, removing the opportunity to learn from them.

> Once you have learned how to notice your emotions, the next step is to examine the beliefs that brought on the emotion.

Do not be distracted by looking at the situation itself. Emotions are brought on by the interaction between your beliefs and your life situation. If you believe that the situation you are in is unfair, then you will feel a sense of injustice. If you believe people are judging you, then you will feel threatened. Remember, your reality is created by your beliefs. If viewing the life situation through this reality is not best serving the life you have been designed to live, then you will experience a negative emotion.

Being curious about what this emotion means to your current beliefs is all you must do. There is no one right set of beliefs. They are different for each of us. Because of this, I (or anyone else) cannot tell you what you need to do with your emotions. You need to discover what you are meant for and what your emotions are guiding you towards. Learning how to use your emotions is the most important part of your recovery.

8

Intentional Living

What you just learned in the previous chapter is the blueprint for recovery—and it's how you will overcome your sex addiction. Addiction thrives in a reality that allows it to thrive. As a sex addict, you have been unintentionally creating a reality that allows this addiction to exist and persist.

Your identity (your sense of self and how other people see you) helped you decide who you are and how the world works. As a high achiever, you've likely lived in an identity that believes you are not enough as you currently are. You want more of anything good (money, attention, respect, admiration, novelty), and less of anything bad (boredom, pain, distractions, failure, monotony). You believed you can create a life that will meet these desires.

Then, the mind comes in to help. The mind feeds your identity thoughts and suggests strategies to help him get more of what he wants, less of what he doesn't want. If your chosen identity does not consider morals, values, or the impact of his actions on other people, then your mind will not consider these things. Therefore, he may get what he wants but end up hurting himself or his wife in the process.

As a high achiever, you spend most of your life chasing more; in doing so, you begin to believe this is the "right" way to live. These beliefs are strengthened with each successful attempt at getting what you want. Every person who praises you for your accomplishments will reinforce this way of life. Because you hide the parts of you that you don't want people to see, your mind is not presented with information that indicates you might be living life the wrong way, chasing things that are actually taking you further and further from the person you want to be.

In a reality where all that matters is more of the good and less of the bad, engaging in your sex addiction is very possible. Assuming that you can cover your tracks, your identity will be getting what it wants without any of the negative consequences. In the addict's reality, everyone is trying to get what they want. So, why shouldn't you?

One, the addicted reality is not fulfilling. Every sex addict I have met lives life chasing highs, seeking novelty, and avoiding pain. They don't pay attention to their emotions, and they don't spend time thinking about what this addiction is doing to their legacy. Their way of life is everything but intentional. It's reckless, short-sighted, and narrowminded. Which is why it's so important to have a recovery plan.

So, how do you put the blueprint for recovery into action?

1) Identify the positive emotions you want to feel.

2) Define what reality you would have to create for these emotions to occur.

3) Determine what kind of person would be able to create this reality. What do they value? What do they believe about themselves? What do they believe about others? How do they use their time? How do they treat themselves? How do they treat others? What are they striving for? What is the legacy that they are trying to leave behind?

4) Once you have that person defined, ask yourself the million-dollar question: Am I acting like that person? If you aren't, then you should not expect to experience life like that person and enjoy the emotions that a life like that produces.

Unintentional Living

Sex addiction happens when you live your life unintentionally. Adopting the blueprint for recovery is the first step toward intentional living, because it's where you begin to listen to your emotions. There's a reason therapists always ask, "How does that make you feel." It's not to be annoying. They know emotions are the only thing you can count on to guide you towards a fulfilling life.

While most people want happiness and excitement to last, they are feelings that quickly fade. As touched upon in the last chapter, those who chase emotional highs are always left disappointed. The higher the high, the quicker it fades. There's no reason to be depressed about it. It's supposed to be this way. Chasing highs will only lead to exhaustion and self-harm. So, you've got to focus on what's important.

Let Your Mind Pave the Way

There are three emotions that are sustainable: a sense of peace, wholeness, and legacy. If you intentionally design your life in a way to experience these emotions, you will feel fulfilled and your sexual compulsive behavior will lose its reason for existing.

To make them easier to obtain, here's how I define these emotions:

Peace - the feeling you get when you know you have a purpose in life—that you were born with unique abilities to help carry out this purpose.

Wholeness - the feeling you get when you know how to use your purpose and unique abilities to make a difference in the world.

Legacy - the feeling you get when you know your life is making an impact on others and the world will be a better place because of it.

Experiencing all three of these emotions and keeping them around is a full-time job. The world is full of distractions and material things that will capture your attention. Capitalism always has a way of sucking you into the abyss of wanting more. There's nothing wrong with wanting more—as long as you are after more peace, wholeness, and legacy.

To stay on track, go back to your blueprint and ask yourself a few questions: *what reality would I need for these emotions to occur? What kind of person would I need to be?* Then make it your reality.

That may sound a little far-fetched, but whoever you decide "you are," your mind will help you become. Think about it. In the past, as a high achiever with a sex addiction, you probably chose an identity that sounded something like this:

"I am someone who needs more attention."

"I am someone who hasn't accomplished enough yet."

"I am someone who needs to do more and then I will be admired and respected."

And what happened? Chances are good, you received more attention; you became more successful, more admired, more respected. This is how the mind works. It helps you get what you want.

Now, imagine your identity if it sounded more like this:

"I am someone with unique gifts and talents, and I wish to use them to help more people."

"I am someone who wants to make this world better for those who live after me."

Your mind will suggest all sorts of ways to discover yourself, to further develop your talents, to search for ways to use them to make an impact on others. There will be no room to act out in your sex addiction, because it would take you further away from who you're trying to be.

New research backs this notion. It shows that mindfulness practices and introspective group therapy exercises allow addicts to self-regulate their addictive impulses and restructure their brains reward processes to support healthy goal-oriented behavior.[33] New group therapy strategies and co-learning models are popping up in the sex addiction space as a result of this new research.

It Takes What It Takes

Process addictions are not like substance addictions. To overcome your sexually compulsive behavior, you must change all of the thought processes that cause it. For some men, these changes will be simple. However, for most sex addicts, making these changes will require an incredible amount of self-awareness and support from other people.

That's why I don't like to put a time limit on recovery. Change takes the time it takes. Some men in my groups change in as fast as four months—those who put in far less effort, take over a year to experience the same results. Time has nothing to do with it. It's all about the plan, and the work you put into that plan. Set up a plan to change your problematic thought processes and keep pushing forward until all of them are removed from your life.

---

33 Eric L. Garland and Matthew O. Howard, "Mindfulness-based treatment of addiction: current state of the field and envisioning the next wave of research," *Addict Sci Clin Pract* **13**, No. 14 (2018): https://doi.org/10.1186/s13722-018-0115-3.

And remember, the world is built for the majority, not the high-achieving minority. This is important to note as you may have to take the lead during the recovery process so that you can help people help you. As a high achiever, becoming aware of your unique thought processes will allow you to better seek the help you need to get sober.

You will also need to protect yourself from yourself. You have a unique skill set that can make you wildly successful financially, but that doesn't translate to inner success. As a high achiever, you need to define the difference between success in capitalism and success in life. There is a way to have both, but first you must make sure that you do not have conflicting beliefs. If, inside your head, success in capitalism is competing against success in life, you will inevitably make the wrong choice at some point or another.

Again, recovery has very little to do with sex and pornography. Compulsive sexual behaviors happen in a reality that is unintentionally created. When you learn how to design your life intentionally, you will experience the world in an entirely different way. When you stop chasing highs, you can create a life that results in feelings of peace, a sense of wholeness, and ownership over your legacy. Sex addiction cannot survive in such a deeply fulfilling environment.

Recovery Should Be Fun

Your recovery is not a burden. It's the fulfilling life that you have been working so hard to create. This addiction will wreak havoc on your life, but it's the havoc that prompts change. Repeated episodes of havoc are what finally make you realize you do have a problem, and you do need help.

One of the sure ways to fail in your recovery is to be in a position where it feels like a burden. Too many men treat recovery like a problem that needs to be solved. They believe seeing a therapist weekly and going to 12-step meetings twice a week will cure them. That's not how recovery works.

There was once a time where you did not use sex, porn, or affairs as a part of your life's recipe. Recovery is about getting back to that point and starting over again. Simply going to therapy once a week and attending a few 12-step meetings are not enough. Process addiction cannot be treated by anything outside of yourself. You are the only one who can change your thought processes.

This is where most men fail in recovery. They think doing the steps as outlined in sex addiction books, on podcasts, or by their therapist will result in a full recovery. But the recommended steps are just recommended steps.

> In the end, you need to become aware of your problematic thinking and do something to change it. Yes, therapy and groups can help with this, but you need a plan, and it needs to excite you. If your recovery work is not motivating you, you're doing it wrong.

The opportunity to live life differently should excite you. If it doesn't... you should be worried. The second recovery feels boring, repetitive, or monotonous is the moment you should start looking for ways to make it motivating again. High achievers hate boredom, repetition, and monotony. When I see this happen, I think two things: one, the potential for relapse is near; two, these men must not know what they are missing out on. If they did, they would be motivated as hell to accelerate their recovery so that they can experience living their life rather than living in it.

Your New Life

For most men, life in recovery is better than anything they have ever experienced. What addiction steals from people is far bigger than it appears. The compulsive sexual behavior is hurtful, but the mental state that allows the behaviors to occur is far more damaging. It harms relationships, your integrity, your ability to deeply connect with yourself and others, and your ability to leave a legacy that you are proud of. While life in recovery is amazing for the men who can get there, this is still an addiction; you need to brace yourself for some of the potential difficulties that addiction presents.

It's frustrating to be an addict. It's like someone else is living your life and forcing you to do things you don't want to do. For those who have not struggled with a process addiction before, it's difficult to understand what it's like to be someone struggling with sexually compulsive behavior. For this reason, you will often feel misunderstood. Because you are not injecting, drinking, ingesting, or smoking a substance, people might accuse you of making the choice to act out sexually. But addiction is not a choice. It's a result of living unintentionally.

You are a complex being just like everyone else. Everyone has had different life experiences and has been influenced by the people around them. The result is a complex and unique individual who has never existed before. We each have problems and struggles that are unique to us; that uniqueness is what makes life interesting. However, as a sex or porn addict, your problems and struggles will likely not be greeted with understanding, love, and compassion.

Feeling misunderstood and unwanted is one of the hardest parts about living with sexually compulsive behavior. Culturally, most people are not aware of sex or porn addiction, and they may make judgements about your behavior based on their worldview. If you are married, and have betrayed your wife sexually, it's almost guaranteed that you will battle feelings of guilt, shame, and rejection.

Do not underestimate the effect feeling misunderstood and unwanted can have on your recovery. Isolation and a perceived lack of support is a breeding ground for addiction.[34] While it would be nice to have other people lean in to support you, this is not common when it comes to sex and pornography addiction. You will need to find your own support group. You may be tempted to

34 Laura Roe et al, "Isolation, Solitude and Social Distancing for People Who Use Drugs: An Ethnographic Perspective." Front Psychiatry 11 (2021): https://doi.org/10.3389/fpsyt.2020.623032.

skip or put off finding a tribe of like-minded men you can recover with. Do not skip this step. If there's one thing you can do to increase the success rate of your recovery, it's finding a group of men with this addiction, with whom you can form deep connections.

This can be hard. High achievers typically prefer the "lone wolf" mentality when it comes to solving problems. But as Albert Einstein said, "You cannot solve a problem with the same thinking that created it."

> Guys are always shocked at how effective connection is. When you finally find a tribe of men to recover with, the addictive cravings and urges begin to fade away. Thinking patterns start to change and become easier to release.

If you have found a group, be aware that it's not uncommon for some groups to slowly drift apart. This is a common story in the sex addiction space. Men will meet other guys at their in-person intensives. The group will meet after the intensive for a few weeks only to slowly drift apart in the weeks to follow. Eventually the men find themselves without a support group. Weeks turn into months and slowly your risk of relapse increases.

You will hear stories of men more than five years into recovery who relapse and end up divorced. If you ask them what happened, all of them will tell you they took their foot off the gas. They stopped connecting with other addicts and failed to keep their compulsive behavior top of mind. Don't let this happen to you.

Imagine a Full Recovery

Despite all of the ugliness, hurt, and pain, you will eventually be thankful that your addiction came to light. You would have never known what you were missing in your life had you not been forced to face these demons head on. Previously, you had grown used to the hiding, lying, and self-protection. Little did you know that these practices were preventing you from getting what you wanted most. Still, it can be hard to celebrate recovery when thinking about all the horrible things you have done to your wife. Her recovery is far more difficult than yours and with no reward at the end. You will achieve freedom from shame, guilt, and lies. She's just hoping to feel safe and some degree of normalcy. It's not fair and you probably wish that you could do her recovery for her. Still, living with intention will ultimately benefit you both.

Here's what you have to look forward to in your recovery:

Benefit #1: No More Hiding

It's exhausting when you are always hiding something. Hiding parts of yourself will prevent you from experiencing the fullness of intimate friendships and romantic relationships. The need to hide a part of yourself tells your brain that you would not be accepted the way you currently are. Therefore, love becomes a one-way road. You may be able to pour love into others, but unable to allow others to love you in return.

By hiding parts of yourself, you assume others are also hiding parts of themselves. Therefore, you will have trust issues. When you believe people are not being honest with you, it opens the door to the idea that lying is normal and everyone is doing it.

Deception is one of the worst parts about compulsive sexual behavior. It will exhaust you and everyone who loves you. In my experience working with sex addicts, it is the constant hiding that perpetuates the shame and makes recovery nearly impossible.

Imagine a life where you don't need to hide your behavior or your past. Imagine not having to worry about anyone finding something on your phone or computer. Imagine the peace you would feel knowing that you have been honest with everyone around you and you have nothing to hide.

This is one of the best (if not the best) parts about recovery. Being fully seen by others and being proud of what they see. When you tell the truth, you have nothing to remember.

Benefit #2: No More Guilt

One of the most defeating parts about sex and porn addiction is the guilt—the persistent feeling that you have done something bad. Guilt will eat at you, and it will destroy your confidence in your ability to change. If you are decades into your addiction, you've probably trained yourself to stop feeling the guilt. It's still there—you've simply gotten really good at ignoring it.

No matter how good you are at avoiding it, the guilt will always creep in. Usually, it's when you are receiving a compliment from someone you love. Rather than allowing the compliment in, your guilt will block it. With enough guilt, even words like "I love you" will become hard to hear.

No matter how great your life is, feeling guilty is enough to ruin it. You will never be fulfilled when you are constantly battling feelings of guilt.

Now, imagine feeling proud of your recovery and the direction you are headed. Imagine replacing feelings of guilt and self-doubt with feelings of confidence and a strong sense of direction. What would happen to the guilt if you knew exactly how this addiction works and exactly what you need to do to overcome it?

Living without guilt is better than anything your addiction provided you. The addict brain will fight you on this, but it's true. Recovery is all about living with a sense of pride and being able to look at yourself in the mirror.

Benefit #3: Living in Integrity

Depending on when you developed your sex addiction, integrity may be something you abandoned long ago. It's hard to admit that you lack integrity. Some men believe that their sex addiction is just one small area of their life and that acting out of integrity on occasion does not make them a person who lacks integrity. Yet, how can you be a man of integrity if you are willing to compromise your morals? Think about it from an outside perspective: Can you really trust someone who violates their integrity? Can you really trust yourself?

Integrity is all or nothing. You have either committed to living in integrity one hundred percent of the time, or you are willing to bend the rules when it's more convenient. When it comes to sex, lust, getting attention, and feeling wanted, bending the rules can be very tempting. Often, in the moment, men feel justified in their actions. It's not until later that they realize they have compromised their integrity.

Facing the reality of what you have done can be unbearable. Like guilt, you will eventually find ways to avoid recognizing your lack of integrity. It's far easier to minimize and justify your behavior than admit you struggle with integrity abuse. Know this: It will always catch up to you. I have never met a man who did not suffer the consequences of acting outside of his integrity. Even if you "got away with it," you will suffer internally. Every time that you look at your wife or your kids, you will be reminded of the truth that they are unaware of. The truth will hurt them, but abusing your integrity will hurt them even worse.

Imagine being so connected to your morals and values that your addiction didn't stand a chance. What if your word was so important to you, that you owned up to all your mistakes and made them right; what if you made your integrity such a priority that you inspired those around you to be better?

It's not about perfection. It's a commitment to living inside of your morals and values. We all make mistakes. Integrity is about recognizing those mistakes, apologizing to those who were affected, and implementing a plan that will prevent them from reoccurring.

Benefit #4: Meaningful Relationships

Sex addiction is an intimacy disorder, meaning those who struggle with sexually compulsive behavior avoid the aspects of relationships required for true intimacy. At first, you might disagree (I know I did). However, the more you learn about intimacy, the more you may begin to see there are some areas where you likely fall short.

Many high achievers, trust no one more than themselves. They let others into their life, but they never count on them to meet their needs. The distrust of others is a huge factor that drives men to hide their secret sexual lives. Without honesty and trust, it's hard to feel safe. And without safety, it's impossible to be vulnerable. But true intimacy requires honesty, safety, trust, and vulnerability.[35] Once you learn this, you will become open to the idea that you may have an intimacy disorder.

It's not uncommon for high achievers to unconsciously avoid intimacy. They often put themselves in positions of power and leadership to avoid being equal. Because of their success, these men have the tendency to make excuses in their head about how few people could understand what it's like to be them.

As Sherry Gaba writes, "Most love avoidant people are very defensive about their inability to connect and to have a healthy relationship. They are often in denial and use anger and defensiveness as a further barrier to creating emotional intimacy and connection."[36]

Perhaps you think that's not your problem. You are good at connecting with people. Like most high achievers, you have developed charisma and people pleasing

---

35 "The Intimacy Pyramid: Creating Connections That Stand the Test of Time," *Intimacy Pyramid*, accessed September 18, 2024, https://intimacypyramid.com.

36 Sherry Gaba and Beth Adelman, *Love Smacked: How to Stop the Cycle of Relationship Addiction and Codependency to Find Everlasting Love* (Authors Place Press, 2020).

skills. To you, and everyone around you, it appears that you are a connected individual.

But in your sex addiction recovery work, you will likely realize that your intimacy issues are depriving you of deep meaningful relationships. As a matter of fact, hunger for intimacy may be what drives your success in business. The story in your head may be that with enough success, women will want to be with you, and men will want to be around you. In a lot of ways, that's true. Career success does lead to all sorts of new and exciting relationships. But these relationships are not rooted in connection and intimacy.

Why? According to Gaba, "Distrust in the safety of relationships is often at the heart of the issue when a person is love avoidant. Learning to trust themselves is the first step." So, while you may think you trust yourself when it comes to relationships, you never truly give yourself to another person. You always keep one foot in and one foot out.

This transient approach to relationships prevents you from ever having deeply connected friendships or relationships. But if you allow it, your recovery will force you into intimate relationships. Overcoming compulsive sexual behavior requires honesty with yourself, your therapists, the other men in your recovery group, and your spouse/partner. Hiding anything or holding back will prevent you from changing.

Assuming that you have found a group of men to recover with and a therapist who understands your compulsivity, you will begin to feel a sense of safety. This is when trust will begin to form.

Imagine feeling accepted and understood. Imagine being able to share more vulnerably with others. Your desire to recover will force you to surrender to the process. The neat thing about recovery is that it's not about fixing you. You are not broken. Nothing needs to be fixed. The recovery process is about feeling seen, heard, and supported. Once you let connection happen, you will never want to go back to the old ways of isolation.

Benefit #5: A Legacy You Are Proud Of

One of the things that is not often discussed in the sex addiction space is the impact this addiction can have on your legacy. Even if you can hide your behavior from others, you still know what you're doing—and what people would think if they found out. Hence, the reason you continue to hide it.

Neurosurgeon and author, Don Miguel Ruiz suggests, "The only true sin, is a sin against self."[37] We all make mistakes and learn from them. There's no sin in learning life's lessons. But to continue making the same mistake, even when you know better, is a sin against self. A sin that will eat at you until it is resolved. This quote from Don Miguel sums up the life of a sex and porn addict. There are a lot of things that are easy to forgive. However, concealing and deceiving others is not one of those things. It will be hard for others to forgive you, and it will be hard for you to forgive yourself.

Having worked with hundreds of high achievers who struggle with sexually compulsive behavior, I can tell you that no one—God, your wife, your kids—will be enough to get you sober. The interesting thing is, the moment you introduce the concept of legacy, your sober mind begins to work. As selfish as it sounds, it makes a lot of sense. What could be more important than how you choose to spend your life?

High achievers tend to care very deeply about their legacy. In my experience working with ambitious men, nothing motivates them more than knowing their life made a difference and they made the world a better place.

---

37   Don Miguel Ruiz, *The Four Agreements: A Practical Guide to Personal Freedom* (Amber-Allen Publishing, 1997).

As Steve Jobs famously said, "We're here to put a dent in the universe. Otherwise, why even be here?"

If the two options are: experience a novel sexual experience or don't . . . the novel sexual experience is going to win every time. You cannot expect a high-high to lose when comparing it to a muted experience. However, if you introduce legacy, you begin to see a shift in thinking. With your legacy on the line, instead of comparing a novel sexual experience and a muted experience, you are now comparing a temporary high and your life's purpose. Put sex or porn next to your legacy and they don't stand a chance.

Legacy is often talked about as if it is something that happens after you die. But your legacy is something that is being left right now. It is the cumulation of your days here that add up to the legacy people will remember. Do you want those days to be full of masturbating to porn alone in hotel rooms, hours of your life spent searching for prostitutes or escorts, days upon days of your life wasted achieving temporary highs? All is at the cost of compromising your legacy.

My favorite author of all time, Seth Godin, defines legacy well with the simple question, "How many people will miss you when you're gone?" He continues to say,

"The best way to be missed when you're gone is to stand for something when you're here."

I'm not sure about you, but my days of wasting time on sex and pornography are over. You have big dreams for your life, and you need every second you can get if you are going to get it all done before your time is up. You cannot undo the damage that you have already caused. But you can make sure that you don't cause any further harm, and you can use your experience to prevent this addiction from ruining any more lives.

Now, It's Your Turn

Wait . . . the book is over? Roland, you didn't tell me the seven simple steps to get sexually sober. That's because getting sober does not work that way. Men all over the world struggle with compulsive sexual behavior. Hundreds of them are getting sober every single day, yet research shows few are able to achieve long-term sobriety—my experience shows there are fewer still, for those who are high achievers, business professionals, executives, or entrepreneurs.

Again, I do not believe this is because recovery is harder for high achievers. But it is different. The bulk of the sex addiction literature and treatment options are written for the majority of the population. But high achievers are not the majority. Their addictions present differently, their struggles show up differently, and their compulsive behavior is driven by circumstances unique to them. For all these reasons, your recovery plan will need to be different as well.

I wrote this book to increase the sex addiction recovery rate amongst high-achieving men. The opening chapters of this book were intended to show you how vast this addiction can be. Sex shows up in our society, schools, friend groups, movies, social media, and in many advertising attempts. When you zoom out, sex and the sexualized female is everywhere around us. I did not write this to scare you. I did it to save you from a life full of slips and relapses.

Most of the men I meet are extremely committed. By the time they reach out to me, many of them have already participated in inpatient treatment, outpatient treatment, and a variety of therapy modalities. The one thing they are missing is a comprehensive plan that they trust to go the distance. Uncovering your past trauma is an important piece, but in the end, it needs to lead to sobriety.

Overcoming your sexually compulsive behavior will require a significant amount of attention, diligence, and dedication. This is not to be confused with recovery being "hard." All I'm saying is that you need a solid plan that you trust and believe in.

What Will Your Legacy Be?

As a high achiever, you are hardwired to fulfill your full potential. You know when you're on track and when you are falling short. It's a feeling inside of your body; paying attention to this feeling is what will keep you sober.

And that will be a big part of your legacy—how you live, spend your time—how you will be remembered.

There was a young version of yourself who dreamed of doing great things with your life. Sex, porn, and affairs were not a part of his dream for you.

You will never realize how much this addiction takes from you until you get sober. Like most men, your addiction probably started when you were young. For decades, you have lived with these thoughts and compulsions. You accepted them as "normal" and never did anything to stop them. The sexual thoughts and compulsive desires got worse as they do for everyone. By the time you were in your twenties, you had to learn to live with them and keep them secret.

It's not until you get sober that you realize how much of your life this addiction has stolen from you, how hours of compromised thinking held you back each day. Over your lifetime, you have lost months and even years of your life that could have been spent becoming a better leader, father, and husband.

It's not just the wasted time. You hurt people. Your actions made this world a worse place to live in. You perpetuated behaviors that harm women and distract men from becoming who they were designed to become. You were a part of the problem, not the solution. You probably wish that you had seen it that way earlier as you know that you would have done something to stop what you were doing.

The worst of it is what was done to your wife. You made her feel replaceable, unwanted, and unattractive; you stripped away her safety, dignity, and trust while shattering her innocence, positivity, and self-confidence. It will be hard, but eventually, you have to forgive yourself for what you have done to her.

> You cannot change what you have done with your life thus far, but you can change what you are going to do with the rest of it. And that's enough.

Overcoming this addiction will show you what matters most. It will show you things about yourself that need to be healed, changed, and sharpened. By uncovering everything that is false, all that will remain is the truth of who you really are and what you were sent here to do.

What you will learn in recovery will change your life and the lives of those you spend time with. As the saying goes, "Your mess becomes your message." This new version of you will become a force for good. You will spend more time thinking about others. You will become more introspective and careful with how you choose to spend your time. You will start looking inside yourself for fulfillment rather than looking to the outside for validation and attention. Life in recovery will be full of meaning, purpose, and intentionality.

The biggest difference you will feel in recovery is in your relationships. As a sex addict, you live an isolated life, looking at other people as tools for your own self gain. Sober, you see the humanity inside others. In healing your own wounds, you'll create space for the suffering of others. Addiction will no longer distract you; you can show up with a level of presence that makes other people feel like they are the most important person in the room.

The relationship that will benefit the most is the one between you and your wife. If she fell in love with the addict version of you . . . she is going to be head over heels for the authentic version of you. It will take a little time for her to trust that this new version of you is the real you and that she will not be hurt again. Eventually, she will feel that this new version of you is not a phase, that truly you are the one she wants to be with.

Marriage will look different. The two of you will be different people after going through sexual betrayal, and a new marriage will have to allow for the differences. You've heard it before, I'll say it again, the new marriage will be far better than anything you've experienced before. For the first time, you will be giving someone else all of you and your wife is going to love that feeling. In this new marriage, both of you will be fully known. True partners in this chaotic world, you'll be supporting each other and trying to make the most of life together.

> So, what will your legacy be?

Will you be the guy who spent the rest of his life chasing sobriety while experiencing a series of setbacks and relapses . . . breaking your wife's heart over and over again . . . asking for another chance . . . destroying marriage after marriage . . . stealing years away from the lives of women . . . breaking families and betraying your children . . . leaving a legacy that you must hide, so others don't lose respect for you?

The pain that this addiction will bring into your life will be some of the worst you have ever felt. There will be times when it feels like recovery isn't worth it. Times where your marriage hardly feels like a marriage at all. But on the other side of that pain is a life that would have never been accessible had your addiction never come to light. The life you would have lived is just a fraction of what lies ahead.

As you choose to live your life with intention, here's a message from myself and the other guys in my recovery groups:

"You've betrayed yourself. You've ignored your moral compass and neglected your integrity. As you look back at the things you've done, you're disgusted by the person you've allowed yourself to become. This is only the past; it's a very small part of you. The future is bright and worth the wait. We have been exactly where you are. Don't let this darkness fool you. All lights turned off can be turned on."

Acknowledgments

I want to thank Dr. Omar Minwalla for introducing the concept of integrity abuse to the field of sex and pornography addiction. His bravery and innovations are benefiting thousands of men and women affected by compulsive sexual behavior. Much of this book was possible because of the things Omar taught me.

I must also thank Michelle Mays for helping save my marriage. Her work is the biggest reason why my wife and I are where we are today. Michelle has shared her genius with thousands of women in the field of sexual betrayal. My wife and I are so blessed to have had her wisdom and guidance in our recovery.

None of this work would have happened without my coach and mentor Gary van Warmerdam. Gary opened my eyes at a time when they seemed sealed shut. Without his guidance, I would not have been able to actualize my full potential.

Walt Hampton is the reason why I have accomplished so much so fast. He was one of the few people in my life who took the time to understand me. Because of that, we have been able to bring some pretty amazing creations to the world. Walt, thank you for letting me borrow your confidence in me until I could find my own.

A big thank you goes to Ann Sheybani for helping bring this book to life. I know that I can be difficult to work with as I'm constantly changing my mind. Thank you for your patience and helping me deliver this book to the men who need it.

I need to thank Gary Anglin for picking me up in a dark time. When my self-confidence was at its lowest, Gary provided me with love, friendship, and a place to live. While it may not have seemed like it at the time, his support at that moment was the only thing that prevented me from giving up.

Many other beautiful people deserve acknowledgment. There are too many of them to name here. I want to thank all of you for believing in me and sticking by my side.

Finally, there's no one more deserving of being acknowledged than my wife. Lauren, my actions made you feel small, disregarded, unattractive, and unwanted. The one person who was supposed to take care of you turned out to be a liar and a cheater. Despite the ugliness, you found enough grace to allow me to redeem myself. This experience has changed you forever and there's nothing I can do to take it back. While our marriage is now more connected than ever, it's hard to be thankful when it was the result of so much suffering. I don't deserve you after all the things that I have put you through. But I am so thankful that I have the rest of my life to prove to you that I can be different.

About the Author

ROLAND COCHRUN received his Doctor of Physiotherapy degree at Pacific University College of Health Professions. He has completed training at the Institute of Sexual Health for Deceptive Sexuality and Trauma Treatment for infidelity and compulsive sexual behavior disorders.

Roland is a serial entrepreneur, business owner, and investor in many industries. While Roland continues to be an authority in the medical field and personal branding industry, his full-time job is running recovery groups for high-achieving men who have developed sex and pornography addictions. Roland has a talent for creating quick transformations and deep group connections. After experiencing one of his intensives, guests agree that hosting small group retreats is what Roland was designed to do.

Tired of sitting in 12-step meetings with people who don't even begin to think like you? Join one of our groups instead, which are designed for high achievers who are willing to do everything required to save their marriage. Recovery is far more effective when you have a tribe of like-minded men to connect with. Scan the QR code here, or visit us at <u>successfuladdict.com</u>

Scan me